Courtly Feasts to Kremlin Banquets

A History of Celebration and Hospitality:
Echoes of Russia's cuisine

Oksana Zakharova
and
Sergey Pushkaryov

Translated & adapted by
Marina George

Courtly Feasts to Kremlin Banquets
by O.Y. Zakharova & S.N. Pushkaryov
translated & adapted by Marina George
edited by Ben Jones

Russian text © O.Y. Zakharova & S.N. Pushkaryov, 2007
English text © Marina George, 2021

Note on romanization & terminology: no single system for transliterating Russian names or other words has found universal acceptance, so we have tried to strike a balance between being internally consistent, yet recognizing those spellings commonly used in contemporary English-language sources (e.g. Wikipedia). We have made no deliberate distinction between Tsar (& Tsarina etc.) and Emperor, despite Peter I's decision to discard the former in 1721, as Tsar has persisted in popular usage. We have generally used metric measures to reduce confusion between modern British, American and other usages, but have included US equivalents in the recipes, and retained some older measures in the narrative parts. In principle, we have also used British terms & spellings, but common US variants are included in the appendix. People marked with † are described in the Biographies, and ingredients marked with ‡ are mentioned in the Notes at the end.

Published by Ōzaru Books, an imprint of BJ Translations Ltd
Street Acre, Shuart Lane, St Nicholas-at-Wade, BIRCHINGTON, CT7 0NG, U.K.
www.ozaru.net

First edition published 1 January 2021
ISBN: 978-0-9931587-8-0

After so many catastrophic events, it would be all too easy for present and future generations to lose their rightful legacy of knowing the cultural heritage of their forefathers. This legacy must always be protected. To remember is both honourable and noble. When memories are gone, they are gone forever.

N.A. Berdyayev

This English edition of *Courtly Feasts to Kremlin Banquets* has been translated in honour of four centuries of the Romanoff dynasty and in special memory of Ivan Mikhailovich Kharitonov, the Head Cook at the court of Tsar Nicholas II who followed the Romanov family into internal exile and was executed with them and their servants on 17 July 1918 at Yekaterinburg.

Acknowledgements
The production of this book has been made possible by the generous enthusiasm and assistance given by many people. The authors would like to acknowledge the contributions provided by the following people: Marina George, whose idea it was to translate and prepare this book, Roy Simmons representing the Orthodox Eucharistic Community in Canterbury, and the students of the Simferopol College for Catering and Tourism... and perhaps above all to all those wonderfully inventive cooks, who inspired Russian cuisine through many centuries. Without them this book would certainly not exist!

Contents

Foreword

When asked to write a foreword for this book, I accepted with the greatest of pleasure.

On each page the reader discovers the history of the great feasts and banquets of Russia, the food that was served and so many historical characters, who added so much to this rich culture.

I owe some of my earliest memories of Russian food to my father Prince Andrei Romanoff, a nephew of Nicholas II, the last Tsar of Russia and the son of my grandmother, the Grand Duchess Xenia Alexandrovna. Having escaped the Revolution, Prince Andrei spent some time in France, after which he came to live in England, settling eventually in Kent at Provender, the family home of his second wife Nadine McDougall.

My father brought with him so many reminiscences of that now vanished life as a member of the Imperial Family and I recall so well the stories about those rich red wines, which my grandfather, the Grand Duke Alexander Mikhailovich, had nursed in his vineyards in Crimea.

When I was a child, I remember my father telling me how, before the Revolution, he would watch the family's French chefs and was always intrigued by those culinary skills of yesteryear. These observations clearly inspired his own innate skills for he was able to produce the most astonishing meals from the simplest of limited resources during the Second World War. Nonetheless, he always relished the Old Russian meals, which would include such things as borshch (borscht) and tyanuchki, a traditional sweet treat not unlike fudge. Such nostalgic delicacies could only have originated in Russia and seem even now to be imbued with poignant memories.

Russian cuisine has always carried a profound sense of tradition and custom, with which I hope this book will fascinate and enrich the reader.

This will be a delightful addition to the library of anyone interested in the culinary history of Russia.

Her Highness Princess Olga Romanoff

Let the banquet now commence with a bottle of a noble Sweet Muscat wine! This photograph was kindly donated by Princess Olga Romanoff, on whose ancestral estate the wine was produced by her grandfather, Grand Duke Alexander Mikhailovich of Russia[†]. We raise our glasses in respectful and nostalgic honour!

A SENSE OF DIVINE MYSTERY

Russian tradition displays an almost religious respect for food and, as mentioned earlier, the Orthodox Church has always played a significant role in social rituals, especially those that involved the sharing of food. The domestic table became in effect an altar for the household, reflecting the holiness of the sanctuary in an Orthodox home. Communal meals would thus be arranged and presented in such a way that the food would be seen as a gift from God Himself, representing as it were, a monastic dining experience, known as a Trapeza.

The table also symbolized the Slavonic idea of the Journey of Life. Indeed, it was where babies were often born and where the dead would be laid out before their last journey to Eternity. For Russians, everything had to have a meaning and even today it is customary to serve a special meal before setting out on a long journey.

V. Vasnetsov, The Tsar's Trapeza. (fragment of the Dinner Menu of 20 May 1898).
Published in "Coronation Lithographic Works by Skoropechatnaya Partnership of A.A. Levinson, Moscow 1896.

Bread, salt and grain – tokens of life and hospitality

The Elizabethan adventurer Giles Fletcher the Elder[†], when visiting Russia in 1588, made the following observation:

> *'At the end of a marriage ceremony, the bridegroom's father presents the priest with a piece of bread. The priest then gives that bread to the bride's father and other relatives, bidding them, in the presence of God and before the holy icons, to safeguard the dowry for the future. All the relatives are asked to keep undying love towards each other. The bread is then broken into pieces as a token of that responsibility. As they have shared the bread together,*

9

so they will share their lives together in unity.' (A.K. Baiburin, A.L.
Toporkov, p. 142)

The Slavs had always considered bread to be the most sacred of all food. In their culture, God gave bread to mankind as a particularly precious gift and when sharing it, one was sharing not only one's own life, but, as it were, one's personal destiny and happiness.

The symbolism of sharing bread was of course inextricably bound with the Christian Eucharist when the consecrated bread becomes the Body of God Himself. Even now, should a piece of bread fall to the ground in Belarus, it is immediately retrieved and kissed, with the words 'Vybachai Bozhin'ka!' (Please God, forgive me!). (A.K. Baiburin, A.L. Toporkov, p. 139–142)

Throughout the Russian lands, including those parts where Muslim culture prevailed, it was the duty of the host to honour his guests by breaking bread for them with his own hands, never using a knife. The ceremonial offering of bread to guests before a meal was a tradition throughout all levels of society.

In the middle of the 17th century, many famous monasteries traditionally sent the Tsar large loaves of black bread made from rye, wheat itself being still unknown in the Russian lands. Loaves presented to the Tsar at the start of the meal would then be distributed among his guests by him personally. Any senior clergy present would be the first to receive this bread and would bow in acknowledgement. Then the nobles would be presented with their share and would likewise make the traditional bow (poklon). Anyone who dared to partake of the Tsar's bread and then betray him would be considered as cursed by God.

Salt was also treated with particular reverence. It was the duty of
the host himself to salt the food whilst the guests poured a little for
themselves straight onto the table if they wished. Nobody would
have ever dipped their bread directly into the main saltcellar. This
tradition refers to the New Testament account of Judas Iscariot's
betrayal (Matthew 26:23; Mark 14:20; John 13:21–27). There is
also an intriguing legend that Christ, when walking on Earth
between His death and the Ascension, only visited those who
poured their own salt, as He Himself was believed never to have
dipped His bread into a communal saltcellar. (A.K. Baiburin, A.L.
Toporkov, p. 143–144)

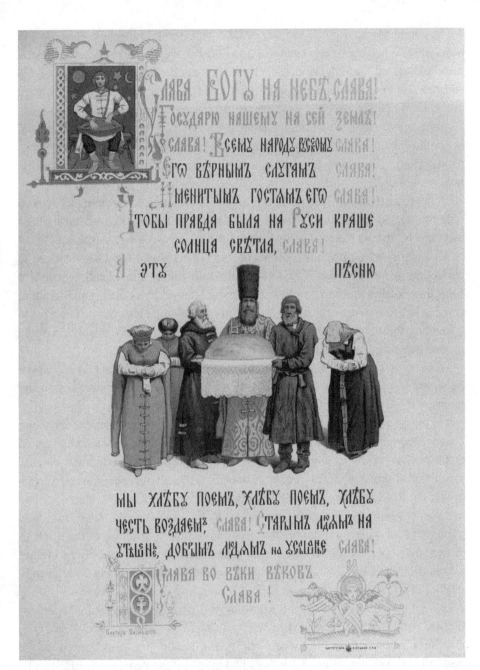

Russian School. "Blessing the bread and salt."
19th century colour lithograph

The combination of bread and salt became an essential aspect of welcome and hospitality. When guests and strangers came to visit, they would be greeted by their host holding out these items on an embroidered cloth. This poignant ceremony is still practised on particular and important occasions such as weddings and when greeting official visitors.

Grains were held in similar high esteem. Kasha[1] (a very ancient and popular dish, not unlike porridge) was mainly prepared from barley, rye and millet. Not only was it satisfyingly filling and warming, but it was also a popular folk remedy for the treatment of colds.

Before Christianity arrived in Russia, kasha was considered a communal symbol of harmony and the leaders of rival tribes would traditionally share it during their meetings to discuss peace. At Christenings the povivalnaya babka (the equivalent of a midwife) would bring two dishes of kasha. One would have been cooked to perfection, whilst the other would have been deliberately burned and over-salted. Both these dishes would be given to the baby's father, symbolizing the fact that nothing in life is ever perfect. The word kasha itself could also be used to refer to a wedding feast, which would be prepared by the family of either the bride or the groom, depending on which held the higher status.

At the trizna or funeral feast prepared at the end of life, a dish called kutia would be served and is still known today. This is a type of sweet pudding prepared from grains, with the addition of fruit and nuts.

It is interesting to note that there would have originally been a strict connection between the rank of the guests at any meal and the parts of an animal to be served. If the head of an animal were offered, it would be considered a particular honour, especially at weddings. This tradition does indeed still survive amongst certain peoples of the Caucasus, and the Kalmyks and Tuvins of Central Asia.

It was not only the food that held special symbolism, but what was drunk was important too. There was an ancient Russian phrase 'piti na niya' (to drink to somebody's honour). This Old Russian custom would apply not only to life but also to death, when at a funeral a toast would be offered to the departed or even to death itself.

The famous Russian historian S.M. Solovyov[†] (A.K. Baiburin, A.L. Toporkov, p. 148) recalled this custom when telling the tale of Saint Olga[†] of Kiev. The Drevlians, a pagan tribe from what is now the Ukraine, had been blamed for the death of her husband, Prince Igor. Olga had invited these people to her husband's trizna, which was to be served at his graveside. The funeral toast could not be refused and the amount of drink served was deliberately plentiful. It was therefore

---

[1] see p.99 and p.171

not long before the Drevlians were quite drunk, at which point Olga exacted her revenge and a general slaughter ensued.

FROM PRINCES AND PROTOCOL TO GUESTS AND GLUTTONY

Many of the earliest tales about the ceremonial feasts of Kievan Rus'[2] might sound quite dramatic but it is important to remember that feasting was first and foremost a symbol of sharing and unity.

It was as such that it would have been understood by Prince Vladimir[†], (c.958–1015), Grand Prince of Kiev and of all Russia. He was not only known for bringing Christianity to his countrymen but also for his great hospitality. The Prince himself would be seen as the first among equals and an invitation to a princely feast would be a sign of deep respect towards a guest, proclaiming that person to be held in great esteem and considered as a close friend.

The generosity of Prince Vladimir extended far beyond any specially selected guests. Leftovers from his feasts were never thrown away and when the Prince saw that his guests could not eat any more food, he would order that the remains be distributed throughout the city.

> 'The passers-by received loaves of bread, boiled and baked meat,
> game and fish... His serving men would simply pour the contents
> of baskets of fruit and vegetables into the shirts and aprons of the
> waiting citizenry. Mead and kvass[3] would be abundantly available,
> the people being able to serve themselves from enormous barrels.
> Those barrels were bottomless!' (P.V. Romanov, p. 27)

Princely feasts were subsequently associated with a great spirit of benevolence and fondly remembered throughout history.

Despite the fact that tables were literally crammed with food, the guests at a feast would be aware that Christian clergy condemned gluttony, not merely as a vice but also as being too reminiscent of pagan behaviour. Those who sat down to eat without washing their hands or praying were considered greedy indeed and guilty of perpetuating the habits of pagan excess and that it was the result of the influence

---

[2] The Kievan Rus', sometimes spelt Kyivan Rus', was a medieval state which existed from approximately 880 to the middle of the 12th century. It was founded by the Rus (Viking traders, explorers and invaders) and was centred in the city of Kiev, which is now the capital of Ukraine. Its polity is considered a predecessor of three modern East Slavic nations: Belarusians, Russians, and Ukrainians.

[3] a special brew made from fermented bread; see p. 104

of evil and heathen spirits. In Russian folk stories, or bylinas, evil characters were always described as being gluttons. One such character, Tugarin the Serpent was always cited by the famous folklorist B.M. Sokolov[†] as being "the poetic image of ancient, pagan excess". (A.K. Baiburin, A.L. Toporkov, p. 155–156)

Ioann IV (Ivan IV) – Ivan the Terrible
Tsar of all the Russias from 1547–1584

Tales of fabulous excess with political purpose

From the earliest times, Russian feasts maintained a tradition of visual extravagance. Guests, especially if they were foreign, would be immensely impressed as five or six attendants walked in bearing a huge tray on which would lie an entire roasted bear or deer, an enormous sturgeon, hundreds of quail, or even just a gigantic, sugared extravagance of considerable weight. During times when sugar was considered a very costly luxury, this was indeed something utterly awe-inspiring.

Each course would be accompanied by a great variety of Malvasian wines and the first dish to be served was always a fried swan. The Tsar would normally send a dish from his table to any visitor whom he wished to honour particularly. Any guest thus favoured would bow deeply. Conversation was always lively amongst the diners, who would have been eating with the silver spoons that had become popular in Russia by the end of the 10th century. Dinner proceeded with all due pomp, pageantry and of course much political intrigue, all of which would be subject to a very strict etiquette.

The head of a sheep or pig boiled in spiced water, and served with horseradish mixed with sour cream, would be reserved for the most auspicious guests. These favoured patrons would then be entitled to cut pieces of meat off the head and present them to those whom they in turn wished to honour for reasons often originating in some bureaucratic intrigue or other.

In the earliest times, food would be served on clay or wooden platters but by the 16th century guests were eating and drinking from vessels and dishes made of gold and silver.

In those days, knives were quite large and very sharp, with pointed ends that made it easy to extract the marrow from the bones. These implements bore little resemblance to their streamlined modern counterparts. Napkins would remain unknown until the late 17th century. At the court of Peter the Great, cabbage leaves would sometimes be placed on the table to be used in the same way as napkins. The boyars, members of the highest rank at the Court and forerunners of the later aristocracy, were often known to use their spectacular beards as napkins – where the aroma of the food would be preserved until their next visit to the banya, the traditional Russian sauna and steam bath.

The Tsar's dinners could well be served by as many as two or three hundred people, who would be dressed in brocade robes, with gold chains on their chests. On their heads would be hats made from the fur of the black fox. To add to the sense of occasion, servants would change their livery at least three times during the meal.

Ivan the Terrible would be sitting alone on a raised dais. The servants would first of all bow low to the Tsar and then go off in pairs to collect the various dishes. At this point the tables only bore bread, salt and spices (especially black pepper and ginger), knives and spoons and, sometimes, jars of vinegar.

It was quite usual for there to be six or seven hundred guests present and there was one occasion within the Kremlin when two thousand soldiers could be seen dining. There were no individual plates for guests; instead the bread was cut into large chunks, providing the perfect device with which to scoop up the food.

Many great feasts, of course, were held to acknowledge special events, such as the capture of Kazan, but very often a great feast would take place without the need for any special excuse, just *joie de vivre*!

In his diary, 'Moscoviae ortus et progressus' written in 1557, Prince Buchau[†] recalled dining with Ivan the Terrible. He wrote that he was not given his own plate, knife nor spoon, but had to share such things with whomsoever was sitting next to him. It was considered quite usual to share like this and it did not in any way imply disrespect. Soup, for example, would often be served in one deep bowl for two guests who would be facing each other, taking turns to drink from this one bowl. This practice was however not particularly attractive to foreigners, some of whom would simply refuse to continue with their meal. As time went by, the presence of foreign guests was taken into more thoughtful account and they were presented with their own individual plates, which would often be changed after each course.

An ordinary dinner continued long into the night and when served by the Tsar, quite often until dawn. Unlike other meals, feasts never followed set times and it was not unusual for a feast to last anything from several days to weeks, even.

One such exuberant event celebrated the Pope's promise to install Prince Vitovt[†] as King of the newly constituted Kingdom of Lithuania, with which Russia had strong ties. Almost every European monarch was invited to this spectacular occasion, which continued for seven weeks.

Boris Godunov (c.1551–1605)

De facto Regent of Russia from 1585 to 1598

The Extension of Formality

It should be quite obvious by now that Russian feasts were not mere dinner parties. They were symbolic occasions, and as such, food was not the sole matter of importance. Boris Godunov, the first Tsar not to stand in direct line of succession

15

to Rurik, arranged a feast in Serpukhov to celebrate his farewell to the army. It lasted a total of six weeks, and at one of the dinners there were five hundred thousand people eating. The tables, set out in the open, were loaded with silver and food. Mead and wine were distributed amongst the guests by the cartload, whilst the visitors themselves were showered with gifts such as velvets, brocades and damasks.

The German Emperor's Ambassador remarked that he could not count the number of gold and silver vessels, which were piled high, like a mountain. Another Ambassador recalled the tables literally groaning under the sheer weight of the silverware. Many items were of an incredible size, with drinking vessels capable of allowing three hundred people to be drinking at the same time.

As impressive as this occasion was, no less remarkable was the reception of the Dutch Prince Hans, the bridegroom of Boris Godunov's daughter Xenia. Occupying a specially allocated place, next to the Tsar's chair made of solid gold, was a table laid with trays, bowls and goblets, also made of pure gold. Each dish had to be tasted by the cook in the presence of the stolnik[4] before it was brought to another table close to the Sovereign where the Imperial Carver would taste the food in front of the Tsar. It was not until after both these tastings had taken place that the food was permitted to be served and the sovereign and his guests could then indulge in their celebration. (P.V. Romanov, p. 26)

In addition to the cuisine, guests were presented with gifts, each one of which had a special relevance and often played its part in some political or diplomatic intrigue.

At one feast, Gospodar[5] Ioann of Moldavia asked Cossacks for help with protection against raids from the Turks and Tartars. At the dinner table Ioann offered food with the following words: "May this meal ease the fatigue of battle and wash away the dust of the road". When the Gospodar removed the cloth covering the dish, the Cossacks were surprised to see, instead of a plate of food, a heap of chervontsy, rouble coins made from pure gold. The Cossacks responded to Ioann "We came here not for gold but for glory, wishing to do battle with the enemies of Christianity" and they refused to take the money. (P.V. Romanov, p. 30)

After the Ukraine had re-joined Russia in 1654, Russian diplomats expressed dissatisfaction to Bohdan Khmelnytsky concerning his country's relationship with the King of Sweden, believing it to be too friendly. In an effort to soften the

---

[4] Stolniks were the palace servants of the Russian rulers. In the 16th and 17th centuries they were young nobles who, amongst other duties, took dishes to the tsar's table.

[5] 'Gospodar' is a term of Slavonic origin, meaning 'Lord' or 'Master'

relationship, the Hetman[6] invited F. Buturlin and V. Mikhailov – ambassadors of the Russian Tsar – to dine with him. The ambassadors refused, prompting the Hetman to invite them again. Buturlin and Mikhailov replied: "Begging the Mercy of His Highness, dinner has been prepared for us at home!" Khmelnytsky continued working to persuade them, by mentioning that their predecessors had never ignored his hospitality before and that the Hetman took the refusal to join him for dinner as a sign that all was not well with the Tsar. The ambassadors did finally relent and despite the fact that negotiations after the feast were very complex, both sides managed to reach a compromise. (P.V. Romanov, p. 39)

The nature of any Russian feast always depended on when it took place. There were many days of fasting during the year, when it was forbidden to eat any animal products. Such strict dietary regulations are practised to the present day by the Russian Orthodox Church.

The Tsar's feasts usually took place at the Granovitaya Palata in the Kremlin. The dishes were brought from the kitchen and arranged in an inner hall connected to the main buffet room where sideboards called postavtsy contained precious tableware that was arranged in the centre of the chamber around a rectangular pillar. Along the walls stood benches with long tables in front of them.

Granovitaya Palata
17th century lithograph

---

[6] the highest military office, and head of state in Ukraine's Cossack Hetmanate

17

It was in the middle of the 16th century that the dinner ceremonies of the Moscow Court reached their peak. At this time, the arrangement of the tables reflected that of the benches in the reception chamber, and the focal point was not so much the throne but the Tsar's table itself. The main guests would be seated to the right of this table. To the left was an L-shaped table, where less important guests would dine. The benches against the wall, which faced into the hall, were considered to be the prime positions. Ambassadors usually sat at these benches, surrounded by people of appropriate status, while their officers were seated in the gallery facing the wall. At a planned congress of monarchs, negotiated by the Lithuanian Embassy, members of the Lithuanian Rada (council) were allocated seats on the benches, and the Polish Rada was made to sit in the gallery. Of course, at this time it was also customary for a newly accredited diplomat to be invited to dinner following his first reception. The number of subsequent invitations would depend upon the political situation and the progress of negotiations.

The serving of food and drinks, known as podacha would clearly demonstrate to each guest their place within the court hierarchy. The podacha was an intractably formal act. The name of each dish would be announced out loud and everybody present would stand up. At dinners in Moscow, the complexity and quality of the tableware reflected directly the relative importance of each ambassador who would be served immediately after the Boyars; junior ambassadors were served after the okolnichiye[7]. Ambassadorial couriers were served at the same time as the children of the Boyars.

At the very height of their formality, the dinner rituals of the Moscow Court could easily last for five or six hours due to the complexity of the intricate ceremonies involved in both the serving of the food and the innumerable toasts.

Alexei Mikhailovich (1629–1676)
Tsar of All the Russias (1645–1676)

Austerity
By the turn of the 17th century, changes were afoot in Old Russia. Rules of social etiquette had filtered down and now their effects could be observed throughout society.

Dishes were no longer sent to the feast directly from the Tsar's kitchen, but instead from a tavern allocated to prepare food on the Tsar's behalf. Men and

---

[7] An old rank and position derived from the Russian for 'close' that intimated a person who sat close to the Tsar – holders of this title performed duties such as arranging travel and living quarters for tsars and grand princes as well as accommodating foreign ambassadors. The position was in use until the reign of Peter the Great.

women were seated in separate rooms at weddings. Women were forbidden from conversing with men and from appearing in public without their husbands' permission, with the exception of when attending church. The man of the house would only present his wife and children to very special guests as a particular mark of respect. Upon the arrival of the guests, the wife would present them with a charka[8] of vodka, only to retire to her own quarters immediately afterwards. A contemporary Russian writer observed "there was often no music at these parties, and even when dancing took place, it was often viewed as something of a joke because it was considered rather indecent for a respectable man to dance".

A day at the Tsar's table

Earlier rules and procedures affecting the daily lives of the sovereigns had become established traditions by the 17th century. Tsar Alexei Mikhailovich, for example, would start his day at four in the morning. After washing, he would go to chapel for a lengthy period of prayer and at the end of his communion he would send a servant to the Tsarina's quarters to ask after her health and whether she had slept well. The Tsar and Tsarina would only meet in the dining room, after which they would attend worship together, which could easily last for as long as two hours. On a couple of occasions, the Tsar was observed to stand in church for five or six hours at a time, perhaps bowing as many as a thousand times!

Breakfast as such very often simply did not exist. The Tsar might instead allow himself a glass of tea without sugar or a small bowl of porridge, before proceeding with the day's duties.

By midday, most official duties would be finished and the Tsar would enjoy his well-deserved dinner. On some days, other guests might have to be entertained, but for most of the time the Tsar and Tsarina would prefer to dine alone, with their children joining them only on special occasions.

Although the presence of guests would necessitate a certain extravagance with up to seventy meat and fish dishes being served, the Tsar himself would only eat strikingly simple dishes.

The Oldest Surviving Russian Menu

A manuscript that has survived to this day speaks of an official wedding party. It describes how the Tsar Alexei Mikhailovich, at his wedding to Natalia Kirillovna Naryshkina on 1 February 1671, was served the following dishes in an area of the room called the sennik[9]:

---

[8] A small drinking vessel, also used as a unit of measurement.
[9] An old Russian term for the cold part of the room

Kvass *(see p.95) served in* bratina *(special ceremonial vessel made of silver)*
Fried swans in saffron broth
Sliced grouse with lemons
Goose tripe
Roast pork
Roast goose
Chicken with lemons
Chicken noodle soup
Chicken in rich shchi[10]

A typical meal for the Palace staff included korovay yatskoy[11] and kulich,[12] while the Tsar and Tsarina were served the following dishes:

'Perepecha'[13]
Kurnik[14] sprinkled with egg
Mutton pie
Sour dough pies with cheese
Larks
Thin blini[15]
Egg-filled pies
Cream cheese fritters
Karasi[16] filled with mutton
Salted-fish and yet other pies

In the days before Peter the Great, beer, kvass, fruit drinks, mead, tea and vodka were the usual beverages for the staff. For the Tsar and boyars, champagne, liqueurs, punches, rum, coffee and cocoa would have been imported.

---

[10] 'Shchi' once referred to all soups, but now means cabbage soup; see p.97

[11] Round, white bread, typically enjoyed with honey

[12] A traditional Old Russian bread, eaten particularly at Easter, and made from yeast and sweet dough, baked in a tall cylindrical mould

[13] Old Russian word for a celebration or wedding bread that was made from finely milled white wheat, which later became an open-top flour product with pinched edges and filling

[14] Chicken pie

[15] Russian and Ukrainian leavened pancakes, traditionally served with various garnishes

[16] Elongated pies, stuffed with meat or fish, which were baked and enjoyed both in the Palace and in peasants' huts.

Peter I – Peter the Great (1672–1725)

Tsar (co-reigned with Ivan V 1682–1696, independent reign c. 1696–1725), Emperor (1721–1725)

European Culture and Dancing Women

Peter the Great was a very early riser, often getting up at three or four o'clock in the morning. After washing, he would spend some time simply walking around his room and planning the day ahead. After a quick breakfast, Peter was in the Senate by about six o'clock. He usually dined around midday but never later than 1 pm.

A.P. Ryabushkin, Moscow Street on a red-letter day in the 17th century
1885, oil on canvas, 204×390 cm. The State Russian Museum, St Petersburg.

He would enjoy a shot of vodka as an aperitif and then, during the meal, wine, beer and kvass would accompany each new course. The menu included thick soup, a whole roast pig in sour cream, cold meat (usually duck), ham, cheese and a variety of pickles, including marinated lemons.

At home, Peter and his wife preferred to dine alone without being waited on, but it was well known that the Tsar would always rather dine elsewhere, never turning down an invitation! He did however enjoy family dinners in the open air, especially in the palace gardens, which he had planned using considerable time and resources and had named in honour of his wife Catherine.

Peter was immensely proud of the fact that his own lands could supply splendid fresh vegetables, fruit and berries, often collected by the Empress herself accompanied by her children. The grounds later became known as the Summer Gardens.

Emperor Leopold hosting ambassadors from Moscow
Etching. 1698. Illustration from Niva magazine.

On 19 February 1699, at the Lefortovo Palace in Moscow, the finale of the farewell reception for the Brandenburg Ambassador was a particularly noteworthy affair. Peter the Great raised the status of women and at this reception the female contingent was allowed to participate for the very first time. There was loud rejoicing and much dancing, while from the adjacent room, the eight-year-old Tsarevich Alexei and the Tsar's sister Natalia Alexeyevna peeped through heavy curtains at the magnificent scene. The Secretary of the Austrian Embassy, Johann Curb, wrote in his diary that 'this was a day that had seen a great break in the Russian tradition, as never before had any females been permitted at public events or celebratory feasts; not only had this been allowed, but women had also taken part in the dancing that followed the feasts'.

F. Bergholz[†] was a diarist who was in the retinue of Charles Frederick, the Duke of Holstein-Gottorp, who had arrived at St Petersburg to ask for the hand of Anna Petrovna, daughter of Peter the Great. He also left this colourful description of the wedding between Princess Lobanova and Count Pushkin that took place in the 1720s.

> *"According to tradition, a Marshal would be chosen from the honourable guests to lead the proceedings and to whom the best man would be subordinate. After the church ceremony, the Marshal would meet the newly-weds and direct them to the canopied feast. The awning of the bride would be decorated with*

the same wreaths that could be seen adorning the heads of the bridesmaids. Two tables were laid out: one for the bridegroom and his men and one for the bride and her ladies. Dinner began after a prayer had been said and once the meal was completed, the Marshal and the bride opened the ball with a polonaise[17]. The ball finished at 11 pm with special ceremonial dances and a farewell to the newly-weds. After completing several rounds of dancing, the Marshal, followed by the bride and bridegroom, their relatives

A.F. Zubov, Wedding party of Peter I and Catherine, 1712.
Sheet from an album in the State Archive of the Russian Federation (GARF).

---

[17] A Polish dance in ¾ time for carnival style parties. Its name is French for 'Polish' and music with the notation 'alla polacca' (i.e. the finale of Frederic Chopin's Variations on '*Là ci darem la mano*') should be played in the rhythm and character of a Polonaise. The Russian composer Pyotr Ilyich Tchaikovsky (1840–1893) wrote many pieces of music to the rhythm of the Polonaise. Tsar Alexander III was a huge fan of Tchaikovsky's music and gave the composer a lifelong pension.

and all the guests, with the exception of any bachelors, would go with burning torches to the bride's bedroom, where everyone was offered sweetmeats". (O.Y. Zakharova, p. 112–113)

At the assemblies of Peter the Great, guests would be offered tea, coffee, almond milk and jam, whilst wine and beer were available only to the men. Lemonade and chocolate were considered to be rare luxuries and were served exclusively at special balls such as those of the Duke of Holstein-Gottorp and his minister, Bassevitz. The host would not dare to force his guests to drink or eat, instead only notifying the guests of what was on offer and then giving them full freedom of choice. Everyone could either dance or just watch. Bergholz remembers that 'anyone could ask for wine, beer, vodka, tea or coffee and would immediately get what he requested'.

Celebration of a wedding and a masquerade in St Petersburg (on the occasion of the *Peace Treaty of Nystad* – 10 September 1721)
18th century lithograph from Niva magazine, 1908.

24

Anna Ioanovna (1693–1740)

Empress and Autocrat of All the Russias (1730–1740)

A Return to Splendour

In the early 18th century, table settings changed considerably. Now there were plenty of knives, forks and plates. At the serving of dinner, coffee and tea, sets of expensive silver and porcelain appeared consisting of cups, saucers, sugar bowls, milk jugs, teapots and coffee pots (the latter not known in Russia before Peter the Great).

Now each person was allocated a set of kuvert (cutlery: from French 'couvert', cf. English 'cover'), which consisted of at least one each of knife, fork, spoon, plate, wine glass and napkin. Tables were decorated with flowers, pomerantsevy derevia (orange trees) and small fountains. At one of Anna Ioanovna's dinners, the table was resplendent with a fortress crafted entirely out of coloured sugar. Twelve large and several small cannons flew the flag of the Russian Empire from its centre.

The celebrations orchestrated by Anna Ioanovna struck eyewitnesses by virtue of their sheer splendour. Particularly notable were the celebrations in honour of the Taking of Danzig in 1734. On that day, the Summer Gardens were already filled with guests by one o'clock in the afternoon. The Empress walked amongst those present and invited them to the table. The Imperial Family dined in a grotto along the alleyway from which stretched a table under a huge canopy of green silk, which was supported by columns garlanded with fresh flowers. Between these columns there were buffets with gold and silver tableware on one side, and porcelain dishes on the other. Before sitting at the table, the men would be handed special tickets and by casting lots, each lady was allocated to a gentleman. Dinner consisted of two courses, translating into a choice of 600 dishes…. And that was before dessert! Guests completed the evening with coffee, tea or cold drinks (O.Y. Zakharova, p. 114–115x).

Yelizaveta Petrovna (1709–1762)

Empress and Autocrat of All the Russias (1741–1762)

Tables to resemble crowns

During the reign of Empress Yelizaveta, the houses of the nobility had special halls allocated for celebratory feasts. In the centre of these ceremonial dining halls would stand a large table in the shape of a crown, a two-headed eagle or a harp, as described in the following account left to us by a guest:

> 'On this day [3 May 1750] her Imperial Highness, by Her Imperial permission and grace, allowed the entire Lifeguard with all the officers to be present at dinner in the Winter Palace of St

Petersburg. The table was shaped like a crown. In the middle of it sat the Empress herself, and the Colonel-in-Chief of all the Lifeguard regiments. Colonels were seated according to their military importance. From this main table, four other tables were arranged as if they were four rays of the sun and at these the officers were seated according to their regimental precedence. The tables were numbered and each seat corresponded to a specific rank.'

Celebratory investitures were arranged annually in the palace. V.A. Naschokin[†] wrote from personal experience that:

'On 30 August 1759, the feast day of Alexander Nevsky, it was commanded that all the Knights of this Order should be present at Peterhof in the evening. After the guests arrived, there was a ball, which started at nine o'clock. When the ball finished, the Knights were summoned to an old hall, built during the time of Peter the Great, where the grand entry of her Imperial Highness was awaited. When Her Most Merciful Sovereign Highness entered the hall, she deigned to allow the Knights to come and kiss her hand. Everybody then went to supper and sat at the tables according to their rank.'

I. Sokolov, Masquerade Ball. 1744.
Illustration from O.Y. Zakharova's book "Secular Ceremonies in Russia of the XVIII to early XX centuries", Moscow – Tsentrpolygraph, 2001.

Yekaterina Alexeyevna – Catherine the Great (1729–1796)
Empress and Autocrat of All the Russias (1762–1796)

Tableware and wrinkles

Catherine II introduced the use of four different dinner services – those of the Orders of Andrei Pervozvanny, Alexander Nevsky, St George and St Vladimir. These would be used for every special occasion. Each piece of tableware was decorated with motifs of the corresponding Order. The Order of St Vladimir service was the biggest set containing 140 kuverts. (O.Y. Zakharova, p. 113–114)

The Empress Catherine the Great was known for a penchant for her French chef's dish known as 'Bombes à la Sardanapal', which contained meatballs made from a variety of game. Generally, however, she preferred simple boiled beef with gherkins or, occasionally, slightly more exquisite dishes, served with a sauce of air-cured deer tongues. Her real passion, however, was sauerkraut in any form. Behind this passion was perhaps the fact that every morning she would wash her face with the liquid in which the sauerkraut had been preserved. She believed that in this way she would be able to protect her skin from wrinkles.

The celebrations of grand noblemen that took place while Catherine the Great was Empress and Autocrat of all the Russias were by no means inferior to the most impressive celebrations at her Court.

Count Alexei Orlov held annual parties for both invited and uninvited guests, and showed immense hospitality to all. The streets around the Palace would be crowded with carriages and the coachmen were each offered a kalach[18], a type of bun, along with a glass of cider. Count Orlov was known to greet all his guests personally. Jollity, merriment, laughter and excited conversation suffused the occasion. These great annual parties would begin after nine o'clock in the evening, with supper being provided for some two hundred people. Count Orlov belonged to a certain brand of nobility, who could not resist large, elegant and exquisitely formal ceremonies. The guests were served with giant sterlets (measured in arsheen[19]) and pike from the Count's own lakes; asparagus 'as thick as a stout stick' gathered from his private gardens; and veal 'as white as snow and reared in his own estates'. In addition to all this, Count Orlov grew peaches and pineapples in his greenhouses, and made a wine from berries, which tasted remarkably similar to champagne.

As could be expected from such a lavish occasion, Prince Potemkin's[†] dinner table also achieved miracles of culinary art. The Prince notably employed around ten chefs, each one being of a different nationality. Below is one of the lavish dinner menus of Potemkin's time:

---

[18] see p.61

[19] A Russian measure of length, approximately twenty-eight inches

Soup made from grouse with Parmesan and chestnuts
Filet à la Sultan
Cows' eyes served in 'Wake up' sauce
Beef cheeks cooked in charcoal and garnished with truffles
Veal tails à la Tartare
Cow-ear crumble
Leg of Mutton
Pigeons à la Stanislavsky
Dressed goose
Pigeons and snipe with oysters à la Noyalev
Green grape gateaux with the finest cream

A. Sharleman, Feast for Prince Potemkin at Tavrichesky Palace. 28 April 1791
From the collections of the Russian State Library of Arts.

As everyone with the means to do so tried to outdo the last extraordinary feast, it became increasingly difficult to stage the truly unexpected but Prince Potemkin managed to present a carefully orchestrated and quite astonishing parade at a celebration for Catherine the Great at Tavrichesky Palace in 1791. On this occasion, the Prince himself served the Empress until she ordered him to take his seat. To enhance the elegance of the occasion, the table at which the Empress was seated was located next to an orchestra accompanied by forty-eight ballet dancers.

The theatre hall where supper was served had fourteen extra tables arranged in the shape of an amphitheatre, with seven tables on each side and every table was illuminated with glass balls of many colours. Other rooms in the Palace contained twenty additional tables, all set with tableware of the finest porcelain and silver. The guests sat in one row facing Yekaterina Alexeyevna, whilst food was distributed by footmen, some of whom were dressed in the livery of the Court and some in the embroidered, pale yellow, blue and silver livery of Prince Potemkin.

> *'In St Petersburg, especially in Court circles, French cuisine as prepared by French cooks was particularly popular. However, a Russian epicurean nobleman would be interested not so much in the recipes of the finest dishes as in the most refined forms and details of the dinner rituals, which could turn any feast into pure theatre.' (Y.M. Lotman, E.A. Pogosiyan, p. 24)*

The hospitality of the Russian aristocracy showed no sign of waning. A table laid for thirty to fifty people every day was the norm. At the table would be sitting not only relatives and friends but also people entirely unfamiliar to the host. In St Petersburg, these luscious feasts were regular events with hosts such as Count Sheremeteff[20] and Count Razumovsky:

> *'One or the other of their palaces was frequently visited by a modest seeker of free dinners, perhaps looking the part of a writer without actually being one. He would of course sit at the end of the table and, no doubt, servants would frequently pass by him without actually thinking of stopping to serve him with food. On one occasion, when still quite hungry, he happened to rise from the table at the very moment his host was passing. Upon seeing him, the host spoke to him for the first time: "Are you enjoying yourself?" The man answered "Very much so, your Excellency. I was able to see everything"! (Y.S. Riabtsev, p. 158)*

Prince N.V. Repnin was one of the magnificent noblemen of the reign of Catherine II. For her birthday he gave a great party for three thousand people, with twenty-five cooks being rushed off their feet preparing various dishes. Liveried noblemen, known for their legendary generosity, stood behind the chairs, serving at table and carving. As Prince Viazemsky wrote "Old Moscow was a stage on

---

[20] see V.S. Sheremeteff [†] in Biographies

which the cream of Russian society would act out to perfection its distinctive and sophisticated life". (P.A. Viazemsky, p. 220)

Pavel Petrovich – Paul I (1754–1801)
Emperor and Autocrat of All the Russias (1796–1801)

Patrician Moscow

When Paul I started his military reforms, he also decided to amend the established traditions inherited from Catherine. No longer were there special tables at meals. The Emperor insisted that only his family dined with him. He himself superintended new kitchen staff and harked back to Alexei Mikhailovich's Imperial desire for food to be as straightforward as possible. He liked simple ingredients to be purchased from local markets. It was indeed rather surprising to see unassuming peasant dishes, being served on luxurious tableware and lavishly decorated tables. Paul often insisted that meals were eaten in more or less complete silence. His Spartan habits, including going to bed at eight o'clock in the evening, were expected to be observed by everybody else. When the palace lights went out, so did all the other lights in town!

It was only after the death of Emperor Pavel Petrovich that those who had chosen to leave Moscow during his austere reign began to return. V.A. Sollogub wrote:

> *'At this point, the old style began to revive with its round of ceaseless and cordial hospitality. This was not quite the same as the life of grand magnates and noblemen such as Potemkin, Orlov and Naryshkin, who often wanted to dazzle with luxury. This new revival was more in tune with that very Russian, spontaneous and generous style of living, reminiscent of the times before Peter the Great.' (V.A. Sollogub, p. 351)*

During the celebrations, young people would be dancing while the older folk would be enjoying themselves at the card tables. Needless to say, tables would be generously laid with food and drink. V.S. Sheremeteff would have arranged breakfasts at the end of the night, after which, perhaps as many as thirty sleighs would be supplied to drive the guests on sightseeing trips all over Moscow. An English visitor J.K. Poyle was in Moscow at the beginning of the 19th century and wrote *'We were swept off our feet by the hospitality and had not a single day to rest our legs'*. (N. Matveyev, p. 80) Another contemporary account recalls an event, to which it seemed that all Moscow had been invited. This was a celebration for the birthday of A.S. Nebolsina[†]. Coaches filled with guests stretched all the way along Povarskaya Street to the Arbat Gates. A rather original present was sent to the hostess by Count F.V. Rastopchin[†]:

*'Having discovered that A.S. Nebolsina had a penchant for special
little pies, traditionally filled with game and flavoured with truffles,
Count Rastopchin sent an enormous pie with what promised to be
a very special filling. Delighted with such attention from the Count,
Nebolsina ordered the cutting of this pie. What a shock to everyone
when, rather than having an edible filling, there appeared the ugly
head of Misha, the famous jester of a certain prince. When he
emerged, he was holding a real pie in his hand together with a
bouquet of forget-me-nots' (S.P. Zhikharev, p. 55–57)*

Emperor Alexander I has lunch during his travels around Finland 1819.
*Illustration from O.Y. Zakharova's book "Secular Ceremonies in Russia of the XVIII
to early XX centuries", Moscow, Tsentrpolygraph, 2001.*

Alexander Pavlovich – Alexander I (1777–1825)

Emperor and Autocrat of All the Russias (1801–1825)

19th Century Nouvelle Cuisine

Alexander I also favoured a certain Spartan elegance, although his was of a more
sophisticated style. He enjoyed French cuisine and preferred surprisingly small
portions, which often disappointed guests. Krylov[†], the author of the famous fables,
dined often at Court and was most disappointed with the insubstantial servings.

Honoured as he was by dining at Court, Krylov was often only too thankful to return home, where his hunger could be satisfied in full.

In the days of Alexander Pavlovich, the organisers of formal ceremonies such as balls, strived to surprise not so much with the abundance of food but with the creativity that went into it. At these events it was fashionable to serve a dish created by French chefs and which was comprised of anchovies stuffed into olives, which were then stuffed into larks. These larks were then placed inside a pheasant, which was in turn stuffed inside a capon. The capon was, itself, inserted into a piglet. This bizarre dish would then be roasted on a long skewer.

Nikolai Pavlovich – Nicholas I (1796–1855)
Emperor and Autocrat of All the Russias (1825–1855)

Chicken Cutlets and Receding Mirrors
By the time Nicholas I came to the throne, the dining rituals had scarcely changed. However, there was one notable newcomer to the list of popular dishes. Pozharsky cutlets!

The origin of this dish can be found within two differing but equally charming stories.

Russians of Torjok

1. The Prince, his chef and the cutlets

Nicholas I was making His Imperial way from St Petersburg to Moscow and went to stay with Prince Pozharsky at Torjok, an old merchant town. The Prince's chef was famous for his veal cutlets, which were to have been served to the Tsar. The chef had however suddenly run out of veal and on the spur of the moment made similar cutlets using chicken instead. The Tsar enjoyed them so much that he asked for the recipe and christened them Pozharsky cutlets, a dish that quickly became very popular with the Russian nobility.

2. The Innkeeper, his wife and the cutlets

The second story has Nicholas I staying at an inn in Ostashkovo where he ordered some veal cutlets. The owner of the inn, whose name was Pozharsky, was alarmed to find he had no veal to hand. His wife Darya suggested that he made similar cutlets but with chicken mixed with white bread and butter. This alternative proved to be so popular that it quickly became very well known on the Imperial menu. Pozharsky himself was so delighted with the success of his recipe that he is reputed to have had a sign made for his inn, which said 'Pozharsky, Supplier to the Imperial Court'.

The culinary brainwave of either the Prince's chef or the innkeeper's wife Darya, gained further notoriety, when mentioned by Pushkin in a letter to Sobolevsky in 1826:

> *'At Pozharsky's, when you dine*
> *On those cutlets, oh so fine!*
> *If you overeat, you'll find*
> *The road could later prove unkind'*

This tongue in cheek comment was a reference to the fact that the quality of Russian roads in those days did not assist one's digestion.

Interestingly, Nicholas I had no affection or enthusiasm for hunting and therefore was never very keen on dishes involving game but this characteristic was certainly not shared by many rulers of the Russian Empire, for whom experiencing the thrill of the chase was generally considered a favourite pursuit.

Throughout Russia local gourmets were full of wonderful creativity and culinary imagination, unhampered by the limitations of locality. The son of Count Zavadovsky started roasting game on bundles of cinnamon and coriander, adding a rich, new array of flavours, unknown in more traditional methods of cooking. Then Count D.A. Guriev[†] acquired fame for another culinary invention, Gurievskaya kasha (see p.158). This was prepared from semolina and layers of the skin skimmed from heated cream. Walnuts, pineapples and various other fruit would be added. This dish was a particular favourite of Alexander III, who was eating it when the train in which he was travelling crashed in 1888 – the famous Borki train disaster, from which he 'miraculously' escaped – and it was recorded that his servant was pouring more cream into the kasha at the very moment of impact.

K.V. Nesselrode – the future Chancellor and Minister of Foreign Affairs for forty years – was married to Guriev's daughter and also had highly avant-garde culinary ideas. With little patience for those who lacked a healthy appetite and who would merely nibble at their food, Nesselrode was of the opinion that food deserved great attention, thought and care. All the nobility of St Petersburg would send their own experienced chefs to the kitchens of Count Nesselrode to learn new culinary skills, a privilege for which they happily paid a high price.

On 13 May 1833, at an exhibition in St Petersburg of Russian manufactured goods, the Emperor arranged a dinner for 500 people in the Winter Palace. When the guests had gathered in the concert hall, the first people invited to take their seats at the table were the Moscow industrialists. During the dinner, the Emperor extended a surprise invitation to eight of these guests from Moscow and St Petersburg to join him at his own table, so that he could discuss in more intimate detail such things as the various levies on manufactured products, the building of the Moscow Stock Exchange and other such industrial matters. At the end of the feast, the Emperor and the Empress greeted all the guests personally, with the Empress discussing with great interest the items on show at the exhibition.

In the 1830s, St Petersburg high society had indeed reached its pinnacle. Including the aristocracy, such as the Naryshkins, the Princes Baryatinsky and Beloselsky-Belozersky and Counts Stroganov and Vielgorsky, the most notable of all were the reception parties of the Yusupovs.

The Yusupov family excelled in highly exquisite taste as displayed at a ball held by Prince Yusupov in 1836. As the festive sounds of the polonaise, cotillion and mazurka filled the room, the Princess Zinaida Ivanovna Yusupova†, with the Emperor at her side, approached one of the mirrors, with which the walls of the ballroom were covered. At that very moment, the mirror started to move, disappearing into the wall to reveal a pathway of flowers. The guests then walked along this fragrant path to find themselves in the dining hall, where another array of novel wonders awaited them. The tables epitomized sheer luxury with orange trees in full blossom actually growing through them. Among these trees and amidst the diamond glitter of crystal, stood vases of Sèvres porcelain filled with flowers, fruit and sweets. The entire display was miraculous!

Celebrations were organized for any occasion, and the Winter Palace became well known for its events. In the 18th and 19th centuries, there were many different categories of dining, and sometimes the nobility would arrange dinners for a close circle of intimate guests without servants. In the depths of many of the great estates there were custom-built pavilions, known as hermitages. These would have a kitchen on the ground floor, and a hall with a dining table on the first floor. The middle of the table could be lowered down to the ground floor by means of a special mechanism. Servants would then load it with dishes and raise it back up. Tables such as these were often in use in imperial palaces, too, and were described by the author I.G. Georgi[†]:

'The dining hall of the Hermitage has, inside its floor, two movable squares. On these stand two tables laid with food, which can be raised or lowered with the help of a simple machine. Each table is laid for six people and is lowered down on order, and then lifted up once again with a new variety of dishes. Servants were thus unnecessary.'

The ceremonial arrival in Moscow of their Imperial Highnesses. 1856.
Illustration from Niva magazine in the early 20th century.

Alexander II (1818–1881)
Emperor and Autocrat of All the Russias (1855–1881)

All Hail to the Tsar!
Alexander II loved all celebrations and revelled in fabulous ostentation. When the Empress Maria Alexandrovna gave birth to her son, Grand Duke Sergey Alexandrovich, a dinner for 800 people was arranged, with due splendour and exorbitant elegance. Being a great huntsman himself, Alexander loved ranging the

forests from morning till night, with a small group of companions. Any game they killed would then be roasted at a woodman's hut and when such a meal was finished, anything left would be distributed to the local peasants. He was especially fond of bear.

The French writer and traveller Théophile Gautier[†] described one of the receptions at the Winter Palace:

'The Empress, surrounded by several high-ranking officials, went up on the small stage, where stood a horseshoe-shaped table. Behind her gold-plated chair, there blossomed a branch of huge pink and white camellia, stretching along a marble wall like an enormous firework.

Twelve tall Africans, each chosen as the most handsome representatives of their race, were dressed up as Mamelukes. They wore white turbans and green jackets, the latter having golden cuffs. Their red breeches were secured with cashmere belts and the seams stitched with embroidered braids. They would walk up and down the stairs of the stage, serving the guests. The movements of these African servants were very delicate and full of the dignity that was typical of their race. Thanks to them, a very European dinner was thus transformed into something of an exotic extravaganza.

At these events, there were no allocated places and the guests were free to sit wherever they chose. However, at the head of the table would usually sit ladies dressed in rich gowns, stitched in silver and gold patterns, forming different figures and flowers, mythological scenes or ornamental fantasies.

Chandeliers sparkled between pyramids of fruit, creating a glittering symmetry of crystal, porcelain, silver and exquisite flowers. This elegant perfection would intrigue the eye, which would then in turn be attracted by the allure of the elaborate coiffures and toilettes. Everything was further enhanced by this marvellous background of flowers, foliage and a blaze of precious jewels.

The Emperor would walk from table to table, addressing a few words to his special guests and perhaps sitting down and sipping champagne before proceeding further. These moments were considered a high honour to such favoured guests.'

Gautier continued with his description of the Winter Palace:

'The hall, with the gold and silver dishes, is neither less significant nor easier to describe. Around the pillars supporting the hall, there stood circular buffets piled high with a whole collection of vases, jugs for wine and water, decanters, goblets, bowls, various glasses, cups, ladles, caskets, beer mugs, stoups, vessels for washing hands, whickered bottles with narrow necks, flasks, pitchers and all that which pertains to the pleasures of drinking and on a scale which could well have been described by Rabelais. Behind these glittering gold and silver plates, were lidded goblets ... and what goblets! Some were three or four feet high and could surely only be lifted by a giant. No imagination was spared in the design of the tableware! Anything capable of being used to serve drinks was liable to be subject to an astonishing, perhaps even grotesque, degree of ornamentation. This might be anything from fat-cheeked Bacchantes and swirling dragons to marching armies and naked mythological figures. Nothing was too fantastic! Through the artist's caprice, vases could so easily resemble huge bears or storks... (P.V. Romanov, p. 144–145)

Dinner for ambassadors in the Golden Chamber. 1856.
Sheet from a GARF album.

37

The Emperor's feasts were administered by the Hofmarschall [21] and his department, all of the officers of which enjoyed a very special rank. The personal chef of Yelizaveta Petrovna was even awarded the rank of Brigadier in recognition of his importance.

The industrial revolution was starting to have its impact on Russia and social change was afoot but pomp and splendour at the Russian Court remained constant, with all ceremony designed to reflect and enhance the great power of the Tsar.

Alexander III (1845–1894)
Emperor and Autocrat of All the Russias (1881–1894)

Hungry Children, Steam Heating and a Russian Wine Library

The Emperor Alexander III had an easy-going disposition and disliked all pomp and ceremony, even referring to himself as the *first* muzhik (peasant). This was reflected in his choice of food, with his favourite dishes being the simple ones, such as shchi and kasha. When drinking, he preferred kvass but he was also very fond of a large shot of vodka accompanied by the traditional zakuski[22] such as pickled cucumber and mushrooms. Every day would see the Emperor following a Spartan regime, both dressing and dining with great simplicity. His children were expected to share this system, sleeping on hard beds and taking cold baths.

The midday meal however could be quite lavish, lasting 50 minutes with no interruption in service, which was a habit adopted from the Danish Royal Family. As the children were the last to be allowed to the table and had to leave it again as soon as everybody else left, it was not unusual for there to be little for them to eat. There is a famous story, possibly apocryphal, which stresses this point rather colourfully. According to his sister Olga, the future Emperor Nicholas II, when a young boy, was so ravenous, that he was reputed to have put his baptismal cross in his mouth and sucked out the sacred relics it contained. This resulted in the later feeling of extreme shame, for he felt he had committed blasphemy.

Alexander loved fishing and would happily sit with his rod for hours at a time. There was a famous occasion, when one of his ministers came to him, insisting that the Emperor should immediately receive a foreign Ambassador. To this urgent

---

[21] A Hofmarschall was a butler with the court rank of 3rd Class in the Russian Table of Rank introduced in 1726. He was responsible for the supply of food to the court, the organization of receptions and travel. He was also in charge of the court servicemen and charged with the upkeep of the dinner table of the imperial family. The Oberhofmarschall was the head Hofmarschall.

[22] Hot and cold hors d'oeuvres, snacks and appetizers, usually presented in buffet style and served before meals.

E. Dammuler, Dinner at Windsor Castle during the visit of Tsar Alexander II in 1874.

Illustration from O.Y. Zakharova's book "Secular Ceremonies in Russia of the XVIII to early XX centuries", Moscow – Tsentrpolygraph, 2001, p.188.

diplomatic request came the splendid reply that "When the Tsar of Russia is fishing, Europe can wait!"

He often changed the venue for his meals, even to the most distant corners of the palace. To facilitate the serving of these whims, special steam heaters had to be invented. Every few minutes, different dishes were served on silver trays, which would be placed on these heaters. The fifty-minute routine was always strictly observed but many a fine sauce must have been wasted! The Court Minister, Baron Freedericksz[†] always thought this a 'gastronomic scandal', but not even his authority was strong enough to solve the problem, as the battle was invariably won by the heaters!

Alexander III's desire for simplicity in everything also reflected an intense patriotism. When it came to the question of wine, he opened the way for what was to become a major advance in the quality and quantity of Russia's own wines. There was now a total change from the days of Alexander II, who was obsessed with expensive, imported wines. Alexander III would only allow foreign wines to be served at receptions for diplomats and visiting royalty. As the quality of Russian wine still tended to be unpredictable, many amongst the officer classes were not exactly enthusiastic about this new arrangement and were only too pleased to dine in restaurants where quality wines from abroad were still easily available.

Prince Leo Sergeyevich Golitsyn was a driving force behind the new interest in Russian wine production. After graduating from the Sorbonne in Paris, he went on to graduate from Moscow University with a Master's degree in Roman Law. This enviable combination of the finest education and financial independence allowed the Prince the freedom to pursue any future he desired. He became convinced that Russian wines could easily compete with the best of their foreign counterparts. He also thought that should a later attempt be made to curb increasing consumption of vodka, then quality wine from Russia herself would attract even greater interest.

Golitsyn was a descendant of one of the oldest families in Russia, and the owner of a famous wine-making estate, Novy Svet near Sudak in southern Crimea. He spent ten years extending the vineyard, planting Chardonnay, Riesling, Pinot Meunier and Pinot Noir vines. In his desire to refine the wines, he built three kilometres of cellars where he allowed his wines to ferment in bottles for three years at a regulated temperature of 15 °C / 60 °F.

In 1892 he received an invitation to accept the post of 'Chief Wine-maker for the Imperial Estates in Crimea and the Caucasus', which included Alexander III's Massandra Estate in southern Crimea.

Having received his invitation, he put forward his own terms before accepting the post:

He made it a condition that he would never have to wear any distinctive uniform nor receive a special title or rank and he demanded to be allowed to do anything on the Massandra Estate that he deemed necessary. These stipulations might have surprised the Emperor but he agreed nonetheless.

When he accepted the position, Prince Golitsyn became the effective founder of a new tradition in Russian winemaking, blending, as he did, art and science to produce vintages of splendid and exquisite taste.

One of his duties was to introduce these new wines to the general public and to open up new markets, which he succeeded in doing. He never betrayed his very high standards, thus allowing his wines to achieve a great reputation as being of superlative quality. His talent for expert evaluation of the quality of a wine earned him the title 'Prince of Experts' when, in 1904, he became the vice-chairman of the Panel of Judges at the World Exhibition in Paris.

This extraordinary ability and knowledge was the result of complete dedication on his part. Prince Golitsyn had a special hall, where he kept different glasses and goblets associated with every type of wine. Indeed, anything and everything pertaining to his passion would be kept in this hall, which was known quite simply as the Wine Library. This dedication to the cause certainly paid off when his sparkling wines won the Grand Prix at the 1900 World Exhibition in Paris and were later served at the coronation of Nicholas II.

Alexander III was always very careful in spending people's money and monitored closely every small expense in the routine life of the Court. During a conversation with K.P. Pobedonostsev[†], the Tsar expressed surprise about an item of expense in the accounts concerning a modest reception at the Palace, at which a surprisingly large amount of fruit and confectionery had been used:

> *'Pobedonostsev replied that such an expense was quite easy to explain. He himself, for example, would eat one orange but would also take one away, as well as a pear, for Marfinka, his adopted daughter. Many guests would do this, taking such a treat for their children as though it were a present from the Tsar himself. The Tsar was actually rather charmed by this explanation.'* (N.A. Yepanchin, p. 179)

In spite of Tsar Alexander's preference for uncomplicated procedures, he nonetheless always appeared at state functions in his full glory and seemed to appreciate efforts, that created humour and surprise. There was one amusement that was especially popular. A large dish of pirozhki[23] would include one pie of particular interest. Whoever came across this special pie, might well have more of a surprise than was expected. If they were lucky, they would discover inside that pie a coin or a ring and thus became the uncrowned king or queen of the occasion.

---

[23] see p.61

If, on the other hand, luck were not on their side, they could well find themselves with a mouth full of hot pepper or highly salted herring! In this case, they would try not to show that anything was amiss rather than become a laughing stock.

Nicholas II (1868–1918)
Emperor and Autocrat of All the Russias (1894–1917)

The Tsar's Catch, Tobolsk and the fated end
The new Emperor of Russia was crowned on 26 May 1896, eighteen months after his father Alexander III's death. The seven thousand guests present at the Coronation banquet included many princes, grand dukes, members of the nobility and foreign ambassadors, as well as a great many people, whose families had made some significant historical contribution to the Russian monarchy. Some of the most distinguished of these guests were descendants of Ivan Susanin who had refused to help the Poles reach Mikhail Romanov, the first tsar of the dynasty and whom the Polish forces wished to assassinate. Nicholas II and the Tsarina were seated under a canopy according to Old Russian tradition and courtiers of the highest rank were serving food from dishes made of gold. In front of every guest was a special hand-written menu. The food served included many of the best-loved traditional recipes such as borscht, spiced stews of meat and cabbage, kulebyaka,[24] fish, lamb and pheasant in a sour cream sauce. Perhaps no one present would remember every exquisite taste, but later everyone would easily recall a scene of great decoration and presentation.

A curious event occurred during this impressive occasion. It concerned the Coronation Cup, a tradition that had been observed for centuries. At a certain moment during the feast, the Tsar would be handed a golden cup filled with wine. Then the 'oberschenk'[25] would exclaim loudly "Ego Velichestvo izvolit pit!" meaning 'May His Majesty deign to drink'. This would be the moment when all the foreign guests and diplomats would leave the Granovitaya Palata. In 1896 however, for some reason or other, this ancient toast had not been declared at the correct moment. This was later seen as a very unfortunate omen for the beginning of what was to prove to be the ill-fated reign of Russia's last Emperor. (A.A. Mosolov, p. 223)

This last Romanov reign maintained all the old traditions and ceremonial courtesies strictly observed for Nicholas II by his Oberhofmarschall, Count P.K. Benkendorff[†]. Alexander III's fifty-minute timetable for meals seemed to have lost none of its appeal for the new reign.

---

[24] Kulebyakas are small pies with a cabbage filling
[25] The oberschenk was in charge of wine and drinks

A.A. Chikin, Evening entry of their Imperial Highnesses Nicholas II and Alexandra Feodorovna in the Granovitaya Palata (Hall of Facets). 1896

The measured elegance of court balls continued apace. Following the first mazurka, Their Majesties would lead the assembly to the dining hall with its time-honoured formal arrangements. The Imperial Family would be sitting in order of seniority, alternating with diplomats and other leading guests from the court, the army and the civil service. In the other halls of the Winter Palace, the guests could sit where they pleased.

The Tsar often followed the custom of moving amongst all his guests. There would be a special chair left at each of the tables, enabling the Tsar to sit down and converse with whomsoever he wished. At the end of the meal, the Tsar would take the Tsarina by the hand and proceed to the Nikolayevsky Hall, where the next official dance, the cotillion, would commence. Soon after this, their Imperial Highnesses might quietly leave their guests and return to their private apartments.

'At the entrance to the Malachite Hall, Their Imperial Highnesses would bid a formal farewell to all those present and then, preceded by the Marshal of the Court, would proceed to the upper floor, where a special private supper would be served to them.' (A.A. Mosolov, p. 202)

An Imperial picnic in Ai-Danil[26]. 1902.

An ordinary Imperial breakfast would consist of coffee, tea, hot chocolate, butter, and an assortment of breads. Ham, eggs and bacon would also be available on request. (A.A. Mosolov, p. 196) followed by kalachi[27] served in heated napkins. It was considered that the best kalachi should be prepared using water from the Moscow River, and so wherever the court might happen to be, water from that river would be sent for this purpose. This was a tradition for many centuries and was especially appreciated by the Tsarina. (A.A. Mosolov, p. 196–197)

At this time another fascinating custom was still being followed, one which allowed Cossacks to enjoy fishing rights in the Urals. A special charter obliged them to send to the Imperial Court those fish caught on the first day each spring. This was called the 'Tsar's Catch'. The honour of presenting these fish to the Emperor was given only to members of the Order of St George. The Emperor would receive the delegation in the great dining hall of the Palace, and the best of the fish as well as some caviar were placed on a special table. The Emperor and Empress

---

[26] A village near Yalta, in Crimea; also known as Ay Danil, Danylovka and Danylivka.

[27] see p.61

would taste these treats and the Tsar would toast the health and wellbeing of the Ural Cossacks. Various delegations would then present gifts, often clocks surmounted by the imperial two-headed eagle. The Cossacks would then proceed to distribute the rest of the food to the Grand Dukes and other high dignitaries of the Imperial Court. Mosolov recalls receiving a pood (about 16 lbs) of superb caviar together with fish, some of which could be of exceptional length. The 'Tsar's Catch' was indeed so great that the amount of caviar presented was often sufficient to allow for lavish presents to be sent to foreign courts. (A.A. Mosolov, p. 198–199)

In Livadia[28], the Emperor and Empress would take breakfast with the whole court. On a special table zakuski[29] would be served and would include caviar, balyk[30], salted herring and canapés together with two or three hot dishes such as ham, dragomirovskaya kasha[31] and even sausages in tomato sauce.

The Empress herself would never eat from this special table as she considered eating when standing up as injurious to the digestion. After this preliminary part of breakfast, which could last for fifteen minutes, everybody would then sit down for the formal part of the meal when the seating protocol was always followed. (A.A. Mosolov, p. 197–198)

At this stage of the breakfast, two dishes would be served: eggs or fish, and white or red meat. At the end of the meal, compote, fruit and cheese would be served. A single footman had to serve those who were sitting at the table, but this tradition began to change as the Emperor increasingly preferred to serve himself.

At eight o'clock in the evening, the Emperor and the Empress would dine. They would first of all greet all those people whom they hadn't seen during the day. Mosolov remembers asking himself how on earth they always managed to remember everyone's names correctly.

Nicholas II always liked company when he was eating. He would start the meal with a small shot of vodka and had a novel way of serving it with a slice of lemon, dusted with a sprinkling of very finely ground coffee and then sugar. This custom is still known and used by many people in modern Russia. After the meal there was nothing that Nicholas II enjoyed better than a glass of port.

In the cellars of the Winter Palace in St Petersburg was a collection of magnificent vintages and rare wines. These were not destined to survive the

---

[28] Livadia Palace was the imperial family's summer retreat in Crimea. The place is often spelt "Livadiya" nowadays, but the palace retains the older spelling.

[29] see p.41

[30] Salted and dried soft parts of large, valuable species of fish such as sturgeon or salmon

[31] Porridge with lots of added butter or mixed with fried onions, mushrooms and sour cream

Revolution but instead were fated to be drunk by the proletariat or hurled into the River Neva in an exhibition of vulgar frenzy.

Nicholas II had inherited his father's preference for straightforward food. Indeed, when he took over the command of the army, he ordered only the simplest of dishes for himself. He once told Mosolov that the war had made him understand that uncomplicated dishes seemed so much more satisfying and that in a way he was relieved not to have to face the rich and spicy cuisine beloved by the court Hofmarschall. (A.A. Mosolov, p. 201)

Alas! This courtly world, filled with rich tradition, wonderful food and yet often strangely understated simplicity would soon vanish forever.

During the exile of the Imperial family in Tobolsk, a telegram from the authorities was received stating that: 'Nikolai Romanov and his family were to be put on soldiers' rations and each member of the family would in the meantime receive just 600 roubles for personal expenses.' At this stage of the Revolution the value of the rouble had diminished alarmingly!

In Yekaterinburg, local nuns brought vegetables, fruit, eggs, butter, milk and cream to Ipatiev House, but these welcome treats were to be prohibited by Yakov Yurovsky[†] shortly before the murder of the Imperial Family.

On 16 July 1918, the day before that murder, Yurovsky demanded that the 14-year old assistant cook, Leonid Sednev, leave Ipatiev House. The cook himself, Kharitonov would die with the Imperial Family.

ENTERTAINING AT THE KREMLIN – 20th CENTURY BANQUETS

The 20th century was a difficult time for Russia. Following the Russian Revolution, the country was in complete chaos and still entrenched in World War I. The Bolsheviks monopolized political power and there were ever more innocent victims of this ruthless clique and its followers.

In the first year following the revolution, the new masters of Russia lived rather modestly in the Kremlin. As time passed however, the 'servants of the people' started to live more extravagantly. The official public style of life presented to the nation emphasized modesty but inside the walls of the Kremlin, a new way of life was developing, which was far from modest. It was very much a case of masters and servants!

The ladies of the Soviet Kremlin were dressed by Lamanova, drove about in Rolls Royces and enjoyed a reputation for being enthusiastic patrons of the arts. At the reception celebrating the second anniversary of the October Revolution, Raskolnikov[†] and Reisner[†] brought from their Volga campaign barrels of black caviar to serve to the Kremlin guests. The humble lifestyle, preached by the new state leaders was being constantly betrayed. Such things were to become a major stain on the 'moral' image, so assiduously portrayed by the Bolsheviks.

One of the first official dinners in the Kremlin after the Revolution was, in its way, as extravagant and contrived as anything seen in the days of the Tsars. It became known as the Horse Feast and took place following a performance of Vasily Kamensky's[†] tragic play Stepan Razin. At this dinner only horse meat was served, which had always been considered a culinary taboo in Old Russia, but, as with so much else, this was just another honoured tradition to be shattered with cynical and vulgar enthusiasm by the iconoclastic Bolsheviks!

Some years later on 8 March 1935, under the initiative of Stalin, a banquet was held in the Kremlin for what was termed 'the progressive women of the country'. The guest list was compiled by the Bolshevik Ideological Department (!) and the editors of the Rabotnitsa (The Woman Worker) magazine. The meal was accompanied by singing and dancing, with Stalin proposing a toast to Soviet women and their heroic deeds. The elegance and delicate sophistication of the mazurka and cotillion of Imperial days had by now been replaced by the proletarian and often brutal simplicity of the harmonica and peasant songs, led by the notoriously ruthless Soviet military leader Budyonny[†]. There was certainly never any danger of a display of Western bourgeois decadence such as the foxtrot.

The destiny of so very many people was chillingly decided at many of these official dinners and suppers during Stalin's time. Marshal G.K. Zhukov[†] recalls political tactics being discussed by Stalin and Beria[†]:

> 'Various situations would be under discussion and certain people named. Then Stalin would suddenly say to Beria 'Lavrenti! Take all necessary measures!' and Beria would then rise and go to an adjacent room to make mysterious phone calls. Names of people would be mentioned; later that very evening they would have disappeared.'

If anyone were heard to say that Stalin was wrong in his judgements, it was more than likely that before leaving the building there would be an invitation for 'coffee with Beria'! The person would never be seen again...

Soviet Russia suffered terribly during World War II, but the hardships caused by that war never seemed to affect the Kremlin lifestyle, and the former Imperial palace was still full of tables groaning with delicacies. Workers and peasants were invited to receptions where they were overawed by the sight of such an abundance of food. Seduced by the allure of vodka, it was all too easy to forget their perhaps superficial allegiance to Communist ideology.

Tatyana Okunevskaya[†], a famous actress of the day, recalls how these official Soviet receptions were very carefully and magnificently staged. They often saw a curious mix of the intelligentsia and working classes, chosen to represent the best of each social level. At the end of the day however, it was much more difficult for the lower classes to exercise appropriate control and drunkenness would become all too apparent:

> *'Members of the ever-watchful secret police would be stationed in strategic places, carefully observing the guests. Once advanced drunkenness was noticed, immediate action was taken. The offender would be swiftly removed from the room before there being any danger of collapsing across the table.' (T. Okunevskaya, p. 136–137)*

Hospitality and Guests at the Yalta and Potsdam Conferences

Endless Vodka, Caviar and International Politics

In February 1945, the Livadia Palace in Crimea was the venue for the famous Yalta Conference, attended by the 'Big Three': Stalin, Churchill and Roosevelt. It was at this conference that the blueprint for the new international scene was drawn up.

Churchill, Roosevelt, Stalin and members of the delegation attending the Yalta Conference. February 1945

The Russian tradition of combining feasting with statesmanship was still very much alive under Communist rule. At 7.30 am on 3 February, the US Secretary of State E. Stettinius landed in Crimea to be welcomed into tents, full of tables laden with hot tea, vodka, caviar, smoked sturgeon, smoked salmon, cheese and a range of breads. (S.V. Yurchenko, p. 164)

Shortly after midday, Churchill and Roosevelt arrived by plane to find these tents still brimming with food as a welcome to Russia. Although Roosevelt declined, saying that he did not need another breakfast, Churchill was only too happy to indulge himself with vodka and caviar.

Staying with Churchill in the palace was the Minister of Foreign Affairs, Anthony Eden and his permanent assistant Alexander Cadogan. In one of his letters to his wife, Cadogan wrote of the generous lavishness of the food provided in their rooms. He was however very uneasy about the continuous serving of vodka and the endless toasts. In his opinion the food was generally very good, if somewhat monotonous; the serving of sweet pasties and caviar at breakfast did not immediately appeal to the English palate. Never daunted, the English delegates soon began to teach the Russians how to prepare omelettes and other English dishes, more suited to the breakfast table.

On the fifth day of the conference Stalin gave a dinner in honour of Roosevelt and Churchill. The banquet was held in the White Hall of the Yusupov Palace. The bill of fare included roast game such as grouse, partridge and blackcock, poultry, venison and elk.

During the meal, Stalin proposed a toast to the health of Churchill, whom he described as a comrade in arms and the bravest statesman in the world. In response, the British Prime Minister described Stalin as the mighty leader of a mighty country, which had faced the full force of the German military, breaking its neck and throwing those tyrants out of Russia. One guest recalled how the dinner, which went on well into the early hours, consisted of twenty courses and forty-five toasts. It is interesting to note that Stalin, as many an Imperial Tsar before him, was to become ever more inclined to opt for straightforward cuisine, as was reflected in the menus for his later banquets.

Political toasts could prove something of a diplomatic minefield. During the supper at the Potsdam Conference, Churchill offered a toast to Georgi Zhukov. In his reply Marshal Zhukov said, "I also toast Comrade Churchill with whom we, as allies, went through this war". Seeing suddenly the look of fear on Molotov's face, Zhukov realized that he had used the word "comrade" for somebody, whom Soviet ideology regarded as a class enemy. He quickly gathered himself together and corrected his words: "For all the soldiers and officers who as allies did their duty in our fight against fascist Germany. For our comrades in arms!" The next day

Zhukov had to visit Stalin, who was luckily in a forgiving mood. Zhukov lived to fight another day! (P.V. Romanov, p. 377)

At the end of the 1950s, the Central Committee of the Communist Party of the Soviet Union (CPSU) decided to restore the tradition of the New Year receptions, in an effort to unite the leadership of the country. Feasts took place in St George's Hall in the Great Palace of Congress in the Kremlin and a welcome was extended to foreign ambassadors, ministers, army leaders, soviet diplomats and party leaders together with their families. These New Year celebrations were legendary in their extravagance, with many exotic dishes such as jellied deer tongues. Food was not the only indulgence on offer as many first-class musicians were invited to enhance the proceedings.

Whilst the fine feasts themselves had made a return, they were not quite what they once were. In 1958 a decree was issued to save state funds, and so the expenditure for a reception was capped at forty-five roubles per person, with spirits being entirely forbidden.

To put things into perspective, at this time a single bottle of good wine would cost in the region of three roubles, caviar and butter costing eight roubles and six roubles a kilogram respectively, and loaves of bread, depending on their quality, would cost between seven and twenty-five kopeks. Forty-five roubles per person therefore could not be considered a particular hardship!

By the 1960s grand receptions were once more regular events in the Kremlin, with two or three each week being the norm.

During periods of much vaunted, so-called economic growth, there was ever the paradox of empty shops and fridges... except in certain circles!

This strained situation prevailed until 1987, when economic and political reforms, known as perestroika, were introduced. Gorbachov brought in a new era of prohibition of alcohol, not only at the official receptions but also for the general population. Priceless vines were destroyed, distilleries closed and Russia suffered ensuing financial losses to the tune of billions of roubles.

As with American prohibition in the 1920s, and doubtless when Nicholas II tried it in 1914, people did not stop craving alcohol. Many resorted instead to quite alarming improvisation, including the consumption of liquids, in which such things as varnish, window-cleaning solutions and brake fluid were involved. Indeed, in only the second year of Gorbachov's ban, eleven thousand Soviet citizens were to die from the consumption of such poisonous substances, all masquerading as alcohol. This was as many people as perished in the entire Afghan War.

Gorbachov's short-lived era of prohibition ended circa 1991.

Plus ça change, plus c'est la même chose

Throughout prohibition the magnificent official banquets continued unabated. In 1988 Larisa Vasilieva, author of *Kremlin Wives*, was invited to attend a Kremlin celebration on 8 March. She wrote of the elegance and lavishness of the proceedings, painting a picture that was especially jarring considering the massive shortages in the shops. (P.V. Romanov, p. 433)

From the beginning of the 1990s the food markets in Russia started expanding, with many products, previously unknown to ordinary citizens, such as avocados, asparagus and capers becoming available. In February 1998 the newspaper Krasnaya Zvezda (Red Star) published two menus next to each other:

Menu for soldiers in the regiment 7456:

Breakfast – puréed peas with tinned meat, tea, butter, sugar, and bread

Dinner – borscht, stew with tinned meat, marrow salad, compote, sugar, and bread

Supper – fried fish with potato purée, tea, sugar, butter, bread.

Dinner in the Kremlin on the same day was:

Fish hors d'oeuvres made of salmon, fresh-grain[32] caviar and Astrakhan balyk[33]
Fried fillet of turkey stuffed with goose pâté
Cream of porcini mushroom soup
Kuril salmon
Veal fillet in a Madeira sauce
Spring salad
Ice cream 'Plombir Korzinochka'[34] with fruit
Coffee and tea (P.V. Romanov, p. 448)

---

[32] As opposed to pasteurized, pressed, dried or unfiltered, all of which are regarded as lower quality
[33] see p.47
[34] see p.112

МЕНЮ

ИКРА ОСЕТРОВАЯ
МОРСКИЕ ГРЕБЕШКИ
КАЛЬМАРЫ ФАРШИРОВАННЫЕ КРАБАМИ
УГОРЬ КОПЧЕНЫЙ
ОВОЩИ

КОЛБАСКИ ДОМАШНИЕ
ТЕЛЯТИНА ВЯЛЕНАЯ

ШЕЙКИ РАКОВ ЗАПЕЧЕННЫЕ В СМЕТАНЕ
ФУА-ГРА С АСПАРАГУСОМ

БОРЩ УКРАИНСКИЙ С ПАМПУШКАМИ

СУП-КРЕМ ИЗ ШАМПИНЬОНОВ И ЦУКИНИ

СТЕЙК-ДУЭТ РЫБНЫЙ

КАРЭ ЯГНЕНКА С СЫРОМ "ФЕТА"

МЕДАЛЬОН ИЗ ТЕЛЯТИНЫ

ВАРЕНИКИ
ДЕССЕРТ "ПРАЗДНИЧНЫЙ"

ФРУКТЫ
КОФЕ, ЧАЙ

———————

22 декабря 2006 года
Дом Городецкого
г. Киев

The original dinner menu for the President of the Russian Federation, Vladimir Putin, during his visit to the Ukraine on 22 December 2006

Menu
Sturgeon Caviar
Scallops
Squids stuffed with Crabs
Smoked Eel
Vegetables
Homemade Sausages
Air-cured Veal
Crayfish necks baked in Sour Cream
Foie Gras with Asparagus
Ukrainian Borscht with Pampushkas (small savoury doughnuts)
Creamed soup of Champignons and Courgettes (Zucchini)
Fish steak 'Duet'
Lamb Ribs with Feta Cheese
Veal Medallion
Vareniki (small dumplings stuffed with cottage cheese)
Festive Dessert 'Prazdnichny'
Fruit
Coffee and Tea

22 December 2006
Dom Gorodetskogo,
Kiev

(Given to the authors of this book by the Service of the State Protocols and Ceremonies of the Secretariat of the President of the Ukraine)

OLD RECIPES IN USE DURING THE REIGN OF NICHOLAS II

It is lovely to sit back and read about the rich history of Orthodox Russia's glorious relationship with food, but the real adventure only begins when you step back a full century and are able to recreate the food that was once served in the Imperial Court.

So, start your fascinating journey here with a unique collection of menus with their respective dates, recipes and historical extracts from books, newspapers and the personal diary of Nicholas II. These will allow you a real insight into life at the Russian court a century ago. Now you can entertain in imperial style!

Konstantin Makovsky, A Boyar Wedding Feast

All the recipes were kindly researched, prepared and tested by students of the Simferopol Higher Vocational School for Catering and Tourism in Crimea, based on banquet menus from the Yusupov Collection at the Livadia Palace. They used the old and authentic methods, together with the decorative techniques that were popular during the last years of Nicholas II's reign. The (sometimes startling!) results, photographed by the students, closely reflect what these dishes would have looked like when they were prepared at the time.

For units or ingredients you may not be familiar with, please see the Appendices from page 164.

17 APRIL 1912

Breakfast

Soup 'St Germain'
Pirozhki
Eggs 'Turbigo'
Fillet of Fresh Water Ruffe 'Mornay'
Mutton Meatballs with New Potatoes
Spring Chicken 'Villeroy'
Apples in Meringue
Fruit Macédoine

From this day in Russian history:

On 17 April 1912 a solar eclipse was seen in St Petersburg and caused much excitement and alarm amongst the people, who swarmed into the streets. The previous day the New Time newspaper had warned people not to look directly at the sun, advising them to buy pieces of coloured glass to filter the light. Those, who could afford to do so, bought specially tinted spectacles and other people manufactured their own protection by holding pieces of ordinary glass over a candle to darken the glass with smoke. Street traders were quick to seize the initiative, charging fifteen kopeks for a piece of soot-covered glass and fifty kopecks for a small piece of coloured glass. This at a time when a pound of beef fillet cost seventy kopecks! A great crowd of people gathered outside the Observatory on the Marsovo Pole (Field of Mars), where they were able to look at the sun through a large telescope...

Also on this day, Russia was shocked by an event, which was subsequently to become known as the 'Lena Massacre'. On the shores of the River Lena, deep in the taiga, 3,000 workers gathered on site to hand in a complaint against management oppression at a gold-mining company, and to request the release of certain comrades, who had been arrested. The response from the management was to open fire on the workers, killing two hundred and fifty of them and wounding as many again.

 C∞∂

To His Eminence, Bishop Innokenty

I am forwarding to you the original letter from the Director of the Museum in Paris, General Niox, together with a Russian translation. Should you wish to pursue the issue of the return of the bell, perhaps you would be good enough to contact the Ministry of Foreign Affairs.

You can obtain further information from the French Consul in Sebastopol, Mr Gay[35], who has told me that the bell comes from the Chersonesus Monastery... The French Government is more than happy to return the bell to Russia as a token of a new friendship between our countries

Extract from a letter sent on behalf of Maurice Paléologue,[†] who was later to become the famous French ambassador, and referenced in Mikhail Lezinsky's book *'Belated insights into European history'*

ഓയോ

Ceremonial Dining Hall of the Livadia Palace. Second decade of the 20th century.
From photographic holdings of Yalta Museum of History and Literature.

---

[35] Louis Antoine Gay (1851–1915), vice-consul

Pea Soup 'St Germain'
(serves 4)

Ingredients:
400 g (3 cups) freshly shelled garden peas, but frozen or tinned can also be used
1 small lettuce, finely chopped
3 leeks, finely sliced
1 tsp granulated sugar‡
1.5 tsp salt
Pinch of chervil and freshly ground black pepper
1 litre (4 cups) chicken stock (see p.116)
50 g (2 oz) butter
Double cream‡ to serve

Cooking method:
Place three-quarters of the garden peas in a saucepan with the lettuce, leeks, sugar, salt, pepper and chervil. Pour in the chicken stock and simmer for 15 minutes. Drain the chicken stock (retaining it), put the garden peas in a sieve and, using the back of a spoon, gently rub the peas through to produce a purée. Mix the purée with the retained chicken stock and then add the butter. Bring the soup to the boil and then simmer on a low heat for another 10 minutes. Add the remaining garden peas and garnish with whipped double cream.

Pea Soup "St Germain"

Pirozhki (with yeast)

From the earliest days of Russian hospitality, not a single feast took place without an assortment of pies and pirozhki (small pies); they had always been a must in festive activities. The Russian word pirog, meaning pie, even stems from the ancient word 'pir' meaning feast.

A rich assortment of pies has always been served although the recipes and ideas have varied through the centuries. Pies were cooked with ingredients such as meat, fish, offal, eggs, vegetables, poppy seeds, apples, berries, dried apricots, cottage cheese, sorrel and rhubarb. Wild rabbit, game and chicken were traditional fillings and the pies were baked with wild herbs like shamrock – known as 'rabbit cabbage' – and kitchen garden herbs such as dill.

There was an incredible variety of shape, size and filling for these pies, each with its distinctive name – for example, kulebyakas, oblong in shape; kalachi[36], shaped like bagels or little pouches; sayechki and shanezhki, both types of small buns, pancake pies or curd tarts. As the old proverb said: 'Anything works when it comes to bread and pies'.

Pies, of all types, could be made with shortcrust pastry, which was more usual, but the tastiest ones were those made from freshly prepared yeast dough.

Pirozhki

---

[36] see also p.46

Yeast Dough

Ingredients:
500 ml (2 cups) milk‡
30–50 g (⅓ cup) fresh yeast (or 2 tsp fast-acting dry yeast)
700–800 g (6 cups) premium quality flour‡
35–50 g (¼ cup) granulated sugar‡
250 g (1 cup) margarine
1–1½ tbsp vegetable oil
1 egg yolk

Making the dough:
Warm the milk and then remove from heat. Slowly stir in the yeast until it has fully dissolved. In a separate bowl sieve the flour, sugar and salt, rub in the margarine and then add the vegetable oil. When the ingredients have come together nicely, start slowly mixing in the yeast solution. Carry on kneading and mixing the dough until it is soft enough to come away from your hands. Cover the dough and leave it in a warm place until it has doubled in size.

When the dough has risen, roll it out and separate it into three or four pieces. Each piece then needs to be shaped into a ball and rolled out by hand until it resembles a long sausage. Using a sharp knife, cut each sausage into 8 equal sections, to get 24–32 pirozhki in total, then shape each section into a ball. Leave these balls to rest for 5–7 minutes before rolling each into a circular shape.

To fill the pirozhki place some filling in the centre of each circle, then carefully join the edges together using a pinching motion to create the desired shape. It is important that the edges are thick enough to ensure that no filling escapes during the cooking process.

Preheat the oven to 210–220 °C / 410–430 °F. Place the filled pastries onto a greased baking tray with the pinched joints facing down and leave to rest for 10–15 minutes.

Pierce the pirozhki gently with a fork and brush with egg yolk; this seals the pastries and will give them a lovely finishing glaze.

Place in the oven until beautifully browned and crisp (approximately 20 minutes).

Eggs Turbigo

The recipe for this dish could not be found in the Livadia Palace archives. The closest reference we have been able to find elsewhere says *"Fried eggs (sur plat), garnished with slices of broiled ham, smoked sausage and tomatoes"*[37]. One theory is that this recipe (and the more famous 'kidneys Turbigo') originated in a brasserie on the Rue de Turbigo in Paris.

Eggs Turbigo

---

[37] *The Menu Book*, Charles Herman Senn, 1908

Ruffe 'Mornay'

Recipe 1
(serves 4)

Ingredients:
1.5 kg (3¼ lb) ruffes‡
3 boiled medium potatoes, peeled and cut into discs

For the sauce:
100 g (3½ oz) butter
10 g (3½ tsp) flour‡
200 ml (1 cup) single cream‡
100 g (1 cup) grated Parmesan
2 egg yolks, slightly beaten
Ground black pepper to taste
Salt to taste

Cooking method:
Simmer the cleaned fish in salted water for 10 minutes. Drain and reserve the liquid. Remove the skin and place the fish in the centre of a greased, heatproof dish. Garnish the edges with the potato discs.
Preheat the oven to 180 °C / 350 °F.
Make the sauce by melting the butter over moderate heat. Add flour and stir until well blended. Gradually add the cream and cook over moderate heat until the sauce thickens. Simmer on a low heat for 5 minutes. Stir in the cheese until it is melted. Gradually add the cooked sauce to the egg yolks stirring constantly, and then return it to the saucepan to continue the stirring until it is absolutely smooth. Season to taste.
Use the reserved liquid to dilute the mixture as necessary and pour the sauce over the fish and potatoes. Cover and place in the oven for 12–15 minutes or until the fish and potatoes are nicely cooked.

Ruffe Japanese Style

Recipe 2
(serves 3)

Ingredients:
3 ruffe‡ fillets
Juice of 1 lemon
75 g (⅓ cup) butter or margarine
2 bunches mixed parsley and coriander‡
Salt to taste
Pepper to taste
60 ml (¼ cup) sour cream‡
1–2 fresh mandarins (segmented)
18–35 g (⅓ cup) mature cheddar grated

Cooking method:
Preheat your oven to 150 °C / 300 °F.
Drizzle the lemon juice over the fish and leave to marinate for a few minutes. Place a frying pan over moderate heat and melt the butter or margarine. Chop the herbs, add to the pan and sauté. Generously season the fish and place in a heatproof dish along with the sautéed herbs. Cover with sour cream and mandarin segments and top with the grated cheese. Place in the oven for approximately 20 minutes; keep an eye on it to ensure the cheese does not burn.
This dish is best served with boiled rice and a squeeze of lemon.

Mutton Cutlets
(serves 6)

Ingredients:
500 g (1 lb) mutton, minced (ground)
150 g (1 cup) raw potato, finely grated
100 g (⅔ cup) sweet pepper‡, finely chopped
2 bunches parsley, chopped
50 g (¼ cup) fresh tomatoes, skinned and finely chopped
Salt and pepper to taste
Flour‡ for dusting
1 egg beaten
Olive oil for frying

Cooking method:
In a large bowl mix together the meat, potato, sweet pepper, parsley, tomatoes and seasoning and roll into 6 cutlets. Cover a work surface in flour and gently roll the cutlets over to create a light coating.

Dampen each cutlet lightly with egg. Place a frying pan over moderate heat and fry the meatballs for around 3 minutes on each side or until cooked through and golden brown.

This dish is perfect accompanied by fresh seasonal vegetables.

Mutton with Potatoes, Greek Style
(serves 4)

Ingredients:
750 g (1½ lb) mutton steak
Salt and pepper to taste
35 g (¾ cup) dried oregano
1 kg (2 lbs) starchy potatoes, sliced into wedges
2 leeks, chopped
50 ml (3 tbsp) olive oil
4 cloves garlic, skins on
300 ml (1⅓ cups) chicken or mutton stock
4 cloves garlic, peeled

Cooking method:
Preheat oven to 190 °C / 375 °F.

Dry the meat with kitchen towel and then season with salt, pepper and half of the oregano.

Place the potatoes and leeks into a baking dish, drizzle with olive oil and add the rest of the oregano. Give it all a mix so that the potatoes and leeks are covered in herb oil before inserting the unpeeled cloves of garlic in between the potato wedges. Bake in the oven for 20 minutes until soft.

Now place the meat on top and pour the chicken or mutton stock over the dish. Put this all back into the oven for 30–35 minutes until the meat is cooked.

Once the dish is cooked, serve on warmed plates, crushing a clove of peeled garlic over each serving.

This is a great winter warmer and perfectly complements vegetables such as cabbage or leeks fried in oil or grilled tomatoes.

Mutton cutlets

Mutton with Potatoes, Greek Style

Boiled Spring Chicken with Runner Beans
(serves 2 or 3)

Ingredients:
1 kg (2 lb) spring chickens‡
150 g (1 cup) onions, peeled and whole
75 g (½ cup) carrots, peeled and whole
50 g (2 cups) parsley, un-chopped
600 g (4 cups) runner beans‡
70 g (5 tbsp) butter
Salt to taste
Pepper to taste
1 bunch dill and parsley, chopped
400 g (2 cups) tomatoes, chopped

Cooking method:
Clean the trimmed chicken and make sure it is secured tightly with string. Place the chicken into a deep saucepan and add the whole onions, carrots and 50 g of un-chopped parsley. Cover entirely with salted water and bring to the boil. Remove any froth and then leave to simmer on a low heat until the chicken is cooked through.

Trim the ends off the runner beans and remove the veins. Wash and chop into diamond-shaped pieces; to achieve this, use a sharp knife and cut diagonally across the bean. Parboil these in salted water, strain and place in a serving dish along with the butter. Place the serving dish in a lightly warmed oven, so that the beans cook through slowly. Remove them from the oven when you are ready to serve.

Cut the cooked spring chicken into portions and serve along with the runner beans. Season to taste, sprinkle with chopped parsley and coriander and decorate with tomatoes.

Apples in Meringue
(serves 6)

Ingredients:

For the filling:
4 eating apples, cored and halved
175 g (½ cup) caster sugar‡
120 ml (½ cup) water
4 egg whites

For the pastry:
340 g (2¾ cups) flour‡
100 g (3½ oz) softened butter
50 g (¼ cup) granulated sugar‡
Zest 1 lemon
1 egg
1 egg yolk
150 g (¾ cup) pearl barley
35 g (⅓ cup) granulated sugar‡

Cooking method:
Preheat oven to 180 °C / 350 °F.

Place the apples in a large saucepan and add 100 g (½ cup) of caster sugar. Cover with water and place on moderate to high heat. When it begins to boil, turn the apples over, lower the heat to a minimum and simmer until soft. Take care not to leave this too long, and once the apples are soft remove from heat and leave to cool.

For the base, place the flour, softened butter, granulated sugar, lemon zest and egg in a large bowl and mix until it forms a thick dough. Cover with a cloth and leave to rest for a few minutes. Divide the dough into two parts. Roll one half of the dough into a long strip and the other half into a circle that will fit the base of the baking tin. Put the circular piece in the bottom of the tin, brushing the edges with egg yolk. Brush the other strip of dough and place it around the edges of the tin, smoothing it out to make sure there are no gaps. Cover with pearl barley and place in the oven until it turns a golden colour.

Once the pastry is cooked, take it out of the oven and remove the pearl barley. Place the cooled apples on the pastry and leave to rest.

Meanwhile, whisk the egg whites with the remaining 75 g (⅓ cup) of caster sugar, until soft peaks form and the mixture stays inside the bowl when you turn it upside down. Spread half the mixture evenly over the apple and place the rest into a piping bag to form a decorative topping. Sprinkle with sugar and bake until the meringue has turned a nice golden colour.

Apples in Meringue

Fruit Macédoine

Fruit Macédoine

Macédoine is a French concoction that became popular with the European ruling classes during the eighteenth and nineteenth centuries. It is a dish prepared from fresh and lightly boiled fruit, soaked in aromatic syrup containing liqueur or cognac and which is then set in a special jelly when cooled, to be frozen with ice cream in a deep, cylindrical mould.

Whilst there are many versions of macédoine, they all follow the same principle, using fruit and berries from any one season. In Russia there are summer, autumn and winter macédoines, and in the south it is possible to create a spring-time version, as of course, some fruit ripen so much earlier in the southern regions, including the Caucasus.

(4 large portions)

Ingredients:
A generous helping of seasonal fruit according to personal taste
500 ml (2 cups) sweet spumante wine or orange juice
450 ml (2 cups) water
100 g (½ cup) sugar[‡]
Cinnamon
Vanilla
10 leaves gelatine film

Cooking method:
Remove the skin and pips from the fruit and berries, and, bearing in mind the size of the smallest berry that will be used, cut all the fruit into equal sizes. All hard fruit should first be lightly boiled in thick sugar syrup (one part water to one part sugar); fruit thus softened will match the texture of naturally soft fruit and berries.

Soak the leaf gelatine in cold water for several minutes, squeeze it out and then stir in a warm (not boiling) water until it dissolves. Mix the sweet wine or orange juice with aromatic spices, the water and sugar and stir in the gelatine. Arrange some of the fruit in the bottom of a deep cylindrical mould, cover with the gelatine mixture and cool. When this has set, form another such layer and continue in this way until the mixture is fully used.

Once fully set and ready for serving, wring a cloth in boiling water, wrap it around the mould for a minute and then turn the jelly out carefully. The macédoine is divided into portions with either a knife or a spoon and can be served with double cream or ice cream.

УЖИНЪ

26-го Мая 1913 года.

———o———

Консоме Селлери.

Пирожки разные.

Мусъ раковый съ налимами.

Соусъ Оксфордъ.

Жаркое: {
Цыплята
Рябчики
Перепела.

Салатъ Роменъ съ апельсинами.

Парфе изъ орѣховъ.

Original Russian menu

70

26 MAY 1913

Formal Supper

held at the Russian Nobility Assembly to celebrate the 300th Anniversary of the Romanov Household

Consommé Céleri
Assortment of pirozhki
Crayfish Soup with Dogfish and Oxford Sauce
Roasts of Spring Chicken, Grouse and Quail
Romaine Lettuce with Oranges
Nut parfait

From this day in Russian history:

I started the day by receiving deputations from 10 am. At 11 am, however, I attended the Divine Liturgy at the Novospassky Monastery. Metropolitan Makary conducted the service, sung by two choirs, those of the Synod and some local singers. After the liturgy we went to the crypt to visit the tombs of our ancestors where a commemorative service took place.

Alexei came to the end of the Divine Liturgy, and from there we went to the Ella community where we were given a late breakfast. At 2.30 pm I went home, received Sazonov and at 3.15 pm, together with my children, I went to the assembly of the Merchants' Society, where a concert had been arranged by local colleges with a gymnastic display for boys in the yard, and a presentation of needlework by the college girls. All this was followed by tea.

I returned home at 4.30 pm and received visitors continuously until 7.30. I did not even have a moment to myself for reading. At 10 pm I went with Olga and Tatyana to the ball for the Assembly of Local Nobility. The hall looked very beautiful. The ball started with a Polonaise – I was dancing with Bazilevskaya[38]. Alix left after an hour. I walked around, watching the dancing and then went to a smoking room. I left at 12.15 am with Olga and my daughters. Feeling very sweaty.

From the Diary of Nicholas II

ɔʒൽ

---

[38] The wife of a provincial leader of the nobility in Moscow

Emperor Nicholas II, Prince Alexei, Grand Duchesses Olga, Tatyana and Maria, Empress Alexandra, and Grand Duchess Anastasia; Yalta, 1913.
From photographic holdings of the Yalta Museum of History and Literature.

Consommé Céleri
(serves 5)

Ingredients:

For the 500 ml vegetable stock:
    1 onion, chopped into large pieces
    1 celery‡ rib, chopped
    1 leek (white portion only), chopped
    1 bouquet garni

250 g (1½ cups) celeriac‡
2 potatoes
500 ml (2 cups) vegetable stock
2 slices wheat bread
1 egg white
Pieces of bacon‡ fat (enough to cover the bread)
5 walnuts
Vegetable oil for frying
5 celery‡ ribs
18 g (½ oz) butter
250 ml (1 cup) single cream‡
Salt to taste
Pepper to taste
1 tsp lemon juice
Sugar‡ to taste
1 egg yolk

Cooking method:
Prepare 500 ml of vegetable stock by placing all the ingredients in a large pan and covering with water. Simmer very gently for 30 minutes to 1 hour. Strain the stock through a fine sieve or cheesecloth.

Next, peel the celeriac and potatoes, cut them into cubes and boil in the prepared vegetable stock for 30 minutes.

Chop the celery sticks and sauté them in butter. Purée the celeriac and potatoes in the vegetable stock, then add the sautéed celery and cream and bring to the boil, whilst stirring. Season with salt and pepper, add lemon juice and sugar. Mix the egg yolk with 35 ml (2½ tbsp) of water and stir into the soup.

Coat the bread with egg white. Cut the bacon fat into cubes and chop the walnuts. Lay the bacon and walnuts onto the bread slices and press. Fry in vegetable oil and cut the slices into croutons.

Serve with the fried bread and vegetable or meat filled pirozhki.

73

Crayfish Soup with Dogfish and Quenelles
(serves 4)

Preparing the Crayfish

<u>Ingredients:</u>
3 crayfish‡

<u>Cooking method:</u>
Simmer the crayfish in salted water until the shells turn bright orange. Plunge directly into cold water and then separate the necks and claws, clean them and set aside to use for preparing the crayfish butter. Remove the remaining flesh from the body shells, then wash them and set aside.

Stock for crayfish soup

<u>Ingredients:</u>
2 large carrots, peeled and chopped
1 celeriac‡
200 g (2 cups) onions
50 g (2 oz) butter
30 g (1¼ cups) parsley
5 bay leaves
180 g (¾ cup) tomato paste
Pepper and fresh herbs to taste
500 g (1 lb) soft fish heads
500 g (1 lb) fish bones
Fish stock (enough to cover root vegetables)
120 g (½ cup) dogfish or other fish (e.g. sturgeon, beluga or halibut)

<u>Cooking method:</u>
Sauté the vegetables in the butter; add the spices and tomato paste and cook together for five minutes. Add the fish head and bones, cover with water and simmer for 20 minutes. Take off the heat and allow to stand overnight if possible, to develop the flavour.

Quenelles[39]

Ingredients:
350 g (¾ lb) dogfish fillet
180 ml (¾ cup) milk‡
1 slice wheat bread (remove crusts)
1 egg

Cooking method:
Soak the bread in the milk. Purée the fish and the soaked bread in a food processor until smooth. Add the egg to the purée and gradually add any remaining milk. When the mixture is smooth, add salt to taste.

Crayfish butter

Ingredients:
100 g (½ cup) cooked crayfish‡ heads and shells from the claws
200 g (1 cup) unsalted butter

Cooking method:
Dry the heads and claw shells in the oven for 10–20 minutes. Break them up with a rolling pin or crush into a powder with a pestle and mortar. Melt the butter and add the shells. Stir continuously over a low heat until the butter turns orange. Strain the butter through a fine-meshed sieve lined with cheesecloth to filter out all the debris. Place the butter back in the pan, cover with some hot water, bring it back to the boil and then leave to cool for 25–30 minutes. Collect the butter from the surface of the water, drain and cool.

Making and serving the final soup
Fill the empty body shells with the quenelle mixture. Simmer the shells, now filled with the quenelle mixture, in stock or salted water for 10–12 minutes.

Using a piping bag, pipe any remaining mixture to resemble crayfish necks, dropping them into a pan of salted, simmering water. Cook a few at a time for 3 to 4 minutes. Drain and keep warm.

Strain the rich fish stock through a sieve and return to a metal saucepan. Add the pieces of dogfish (or other fish). Then add the stuffed crayfish and the crayfish flesh that was removed from the shells previously when making the quenelles, and the crayfish butter, and heat the soup over low heat for 10 minutes. Serve with the quenelles and chopped fresh herbs.

---

[39] a poached oval-shaped mixture of cream and fish or meat, using egg and sometimes breadcrumbs as a binding material

Crayfish Soup with Dogfish

Cumberland Sauce
English cuisine[40]

Ingredients:
Peel of 1 large orange
Peel of 1 large lemon
140 g (½ cup) clear jelly‡ (redcurrant or plum)
Juice of 1 lemon
70 ml (⅓ cup) port (use a bit more, if necessary)
25 g (¼ cup) icing sugar‡
1–2 tsp Dijon mustard
Pinch of ground ginger
Ground white pepper to taste

Cooking method:
Place the orange and lemon peel in water in a small saucepan and boil for 5–10 minutes until soft. Drain and dry the peel, cut into narrow strips and return to the saucepan. Add the jelly, lemon juice, port, icing sugar, Dijon mustard, ginger and ground white pepper. Cook on a low heat, stirring continuously until the jelly dissolves. Take the saucepan off the heat and whisk until the sauce achieves a good consistency. The sauce will thicken as it cools down. To make the sauce slightly thinner, add a little more port. (If a smooth sauce is desired the sauce can be pushed through a sieve). Cover with a lid and place in the fridge to cool. Whisk before serving.

The sauce can be kept in the fridge for one week and is perfect served with cold meats and poultry or hot ham and tongue.

---

[40] Cumberland sauce is a contemporary replacement for Oxford Sauce, the difference lying in the rind. In Oxford sauce less rind is used and the rinds are finely chopped or grated.

Game Dishes

<u>To prepare the game:</u>

If game birds have been stored for a few days, it is easier to remove the feathers by pouring boiling water over the birds first. (This method can also be used even if the birds have been stored in a freezer.)

Following the feather removal, it is necessary to singe the game over a low heat to remove any 'hair' and to sterilize the birds. Before singeing, rub flour into the bird to make any remaining feathers and 'hair' stand on end. As an alternative to singeing, it is also possible to clean the skin with a piece of pork fat‡ wrapped in a linen cloth.

Waterfowl is better skinned completely to remove both the feathers and the subcutaneous fat, which has an unpleasant swampy smell.

When gutting the bird, cut off the head and legs first and avoid any pressure on the gall bladder. The lungs, which are bitter in taste, should then be removed. The heart, liver and stomach are edible and can be used. The bird should be washed thoroughly in warm water to remove any blood clots.

Prepared large birds can be cooked whole or cut into pieces. Medium-sized birds can be cooked either whole or cut into halves. Small game birds, such as snipe, woodcock and quail are cooked whole.

Fried Grouse
(serves 1)

<u>Ingredients:</u>
1 grouse
50 g (¼ cup) lardons (thick bacon‡) cut into pieces
10 g (2 tsp) lard‡
5 g (1 tsp) butter
100 ml (½ cup) game stock
60 g (⅓ cup) salad or marinated fruit

<u>Cooking method:</u>
The grouse can be moistened by stuffing with thick bacon that has been cut into cubes. This method can also be used when cooking partridges.

Place the prepared bird in boiling water for one minute. Salt, and place in a saucepan and fry in lard and butter. Cover the saucepan with a lid and leave to cook on a low heat until cooked through. Remove the fat, add the game stock to the saucepan and bring back to the boil. Serve the bird in the same pan that it was cooked in. Garnish with melted butter and serve with salad or fruit.

At the Russian court this game bird would be elaborately decorated and presented as a reconstructed, complete bird. This is of course not necessary but the Simferopol cookery students have recreated this dish as it was served to the Tsar.

Fried Grouse

79

Quail Cooked in Vine Leaves
(serves 4)

Ingredients:
8 quail
Salted or pickled vine leaves (allow 4–5 per quail)
Salt and freshly milled black pepper
200 g (1 cup) butter

Cooking method:
Salt the prepared birds, grease with butter, wrap in vine leaves and secure with string. Cover with a tea towel and leave for 30 minutes. Then fry in a large pan for 15–20 minutes in a generous quantity of fat.

20–30 g of butter is required per quail.

Pheasant Bake

Pheasant Bake
(serves 4)

Ingredients:
2 pheasants
Pieces of pork belly fat‡
150 g (⅔ cup) butter
100 g (½ cup) speck‡ (smoked pork belly)
200 ml (1 cup) sour cream‡
Salt to taste
100 g (1 cup) wheat breadcrumbs
Extra butter for frying the wings, tail and head

Cooking method:
The pheasant should be stored in a cool, dry place for a few days. It is ready for cooking when the meat becomes soft and carries an aged meat aroma (it must not smell rotten). At this point the pheasant meat is at its most flavoursome and tender.

When cleaning and cutting the bird, do not remove the feathers from tail, wings and head.

Before frying the pheasant, grease it thoroughly with a piece of lard, fill the chest with speck, rub the inside and outside with salt and then fry in butter, continuously pouring boiling water on it at first and then basting it with its own juices and greasing it with sour cream. To ensure a juicy bird, pierce it liberally with a fork.

Before it has finished cooking, baste the bird with butter for a final time and sprinkle with fine breadcrumbs. To keep the breadcrumbs on the bird, leave in the oven for a further 5–10 minutes to dry slightly and then serve.

The wings, tail and head are fried in fat. For this purpose, they are carefully placed into a generous amount of butter, holding the feathers to make sure they stay dry. Then re-attach the head, tail and wings in the appropriate positions on the fried pheasants using small skewers.

Pheasant is usually served on a single white bread crouton of an appropriate size. Small game meat is arranged around the pheasant and garnished with pieces of romaine (cos) lettuce.

The plain stock from the pheasant and the small game meat serves as an uncomplicated sauce.

Pheasant cooked gently, then covered in thin pastry, into which when suitably firm the feathers are replaced, can give a realistic impression. Such would be the presentation of this dish at Nicholas II's summer retreat of Livadia in Crimea.

Roast Capon
(serves 4)

Ingredients:
3.5 kg (7½ lbs) capon‡
Salt and oil
Kitchen roll (paper towel)
100 g (3½ oz) butter for basting
60 g (2 oz) butter
115 g (2 cups) soft wheat breadcrumbs
Fresh green herbs
235 ml (1 cup) red wine
6–9 mushrooms‡
115 ml (½ cup) lemon or gooseberry juice

Cooking method:
Clean the capon, salt, and wrap with oiled paper, which can be secured with string. Roast, ideally on a skewer, basting regularly with butter.

Fry the white bread crumbs in the extra butter and sprinkle this mixture on the capon. Cut the bird into 12 parts, sprinkle with fresh green herbs and cover with a mixture of its own juices blended with the red wine, fried mushrooms and lemon or gooseberry juice.

Cos Lettuce with Oranges and Bananas
(8 side servings)

Ingredients:
300 g (4 cups) cos lettuce[‡]
100 g (2 cups) curly endive[‡]
150 g (⅔ cup) orange, peeled and thinly sliced. Reserve the zest.
150 g (½ cup) banana or apple, peeled and chopped
150 g (⅔ cup) salad dressing of your choice

Cooking method:
Chop the lettuce and curly endive, add thinly sliced oranges and bananas or apples and then pour the salad dressing over. Place into a salad bowl and sprinkle with grated orange zest.

Nut Parfait with chocolate
(serves 8)

Ingredients:
150 g (⅔ cup) dark chocolate (70% cocoa or more)
500 ml (2 cups) freshly brewed coffee
100 g (3½ oz) butter or margarine
6 eggs (6 whites and 3 yolks)
100 g (⅔ cup) mixed nuts
140 g (⅔ cup) granulated sugar‡
200 ml (1 cup) double cream‡

Cooking method:
Place the chocolate, coffee (reserving 2 tsp) and butter/margarine into a pan and melt on a low heat stirring continuously. Leave to cool.

Separate the eggs. Add 3 yolks to the mixture, stir and add the nuts. Whisk 3 egg whites and 105 g of sugar, adding this carefully to the chocolate mixture. Pour the final mixture into a mould and place in the freezer to harden.

Meanwhile, whisk the cream with the remaining 35 g of sugar. Add the reserved coffee and mix thoroughly. Remove the mould from the freezer, put the whipped cream on top of the chocolate layer, refreeze. Whisk the remaining three egg whites and arrange carefully on the top of the mould, which is then returned to the freezer.

When ready to serve, allow the parfait to defrost slightly before presenting.

Nut Parfait with pomadka
(serves 2)

Ingredients:
115 g (½ cup) fructose (if possible); otherwise use ordinary sugar
100 ml (½ cup) water
225 g (1½ cups) walnuts
100 ml (½ cup) double cream‡

Cooking method:
To make pomadka (fudge or fondant mixture), cook the sugar and water together over low heat, stirring gently. To achieve the correct consistency, test the syrup by pouring a little over the back of a spoon into some cold water. If it hardens into fine strands, it is ready to use.

Once this pomadka is ready, place in a bowl and stir with a wooden spoon until you achieve a cream-like consistency. Place the nuts in a food processor, adding slowly 1–2 tbsp of water until you have a soft paste. Add this paste in small amounts to the pomadka, mixing continuously.

Whisk the cream until well thickened. Place alternate layers of cream and paste into a mould that has been greased lightly with butter. Cover with a lid, which must also be greased. The parfait must be kept well chilled for at least three hours.

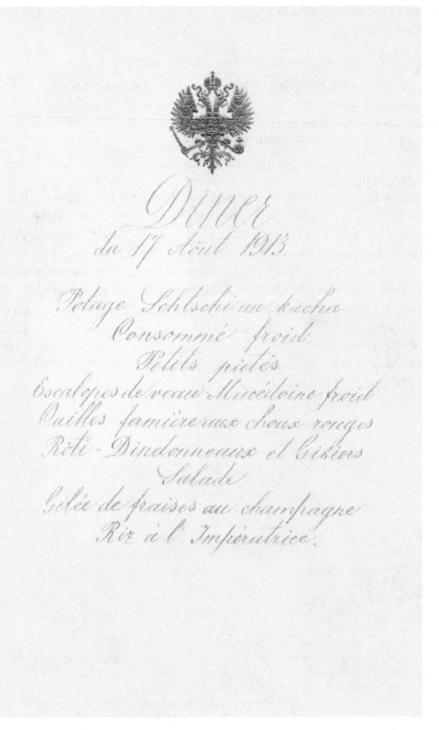

Diner
du 17 Août 1913.

Potage Schtschi au kacha
Consommé froid
Petits pâtés
Escalopes de veau Macédoine froid
Cailles farcie aux choux rouges
Rôti - Dindonneaux et Gibiers
Salade
Gelée de fraises au champagne
Riz à l'Impératrice.

Original French Menu

17 AUGUST 1913

Dinner

Shchi with Kasha

Cold Consommé

Pirozhki

Veal Escalope – Cold Macédoine

Quail with Red Cabbage

Turkey and Game Roast

Salad

Strawberry Jelly in Champagne

Riz à l'Impératrice

From this day in Russian history:

On 14 August, Nicholas II arrived in Yalta with his family in order to celebrate the 100th anniversary of the Battle of Kulm (Chlumec in Bohemia) on 17 August. At this battle, a major attack by crack French troops was defeated, thus setting the scene for the eventual success of the entire 1813 campaign. A telegram was sent from General Bogdanovich to General Yablochkin of the Yegersky[41] Regiment. In this telegram he recalled the many acts of heroism and bravery, which culminated in such a stunning victory. The many stories of the Battle of Kulm would become legendary and an inspiration for many a year. The full and generous text of this telegram was published in that day's issue of the Russian Riviera.

ෆ๛

In the morning, I went down with Olga and my daughters to have a swim in the sea. Wonderful! At 11.30 am we went to the Standart [the Imperial yacht]. Prayers were offered for the 100th anniversary of the Battle of Kulm and breakfast was then served in the mess. We were there alone without any attendants. Then, while I was sitting in the engine room, dancing started in the children's dining room and lasted until 4 pm. We then returned to Livadia, where I walked until teatime.

Read till 7.30 pm. Had dinner with some old jägers and young officers from the regiments that had participated in the Battle of Kulm. The temperature both indoors and outdoors was extreme.

From the diary of Nicholas II

---

[41] His Majesty's Lifeguard Jägers

On the anniversary of the Battle, a dinner was held at the Livadia Palace, in honour of the Yegersky Lifeguards. The Emperor and The Grand Duchess Olga Alexandrovna were present at the dinner as well as the Emperor's Daughters and some other people from the Court entourage. Also invited were officers from the regiments that took part in the Battle of Kulm: Prince Konstantin Konstantinovich of the Izmailovsky Lifeguards; former commanders of the Yegersky Lifeguards; Maltsev, a retired infantry general; Lieutenant General Zionchkovsky; Captain Kutepov, who was serving in the Emperor's personal infantry regiment; Zelenetsky, a Captain of the First Rank of the Imperial Guards; Colonel Sherekhovsky of the St Petersburg Lifeguards; and many others. At the dinner the Emperor drank the health of the Yegersky Lifeguards and of all the units which had taken part in the glorious Battle of Kulm. Before the dinner the aforementioned officers from the Yegersky Lifeguards had the honour of being presented to the Sovereign, after which bouquets were presented to the Grand Duchesses.

Russian Riviera, 17 August 1913

Two views of a Dragoon Guard Officers' banquet in the Vladimir Palace, 1912

Tsarskiye Shchi[42]
(serves 4)

Ingredients:
150 g (⅔ cup) lardons (thick bacon‡)
800 g (8 cups) fresh cabbage
100 g (⅔ cup) potatoes
2 carrots
2 onions
3 parsley roots (or 3 small parsnips)
800 ml (3 cups) beef stock
Fresh green herbs
Salt and pepper to taste

Cooking method:
Cut the bacon into cubes and fry until crispy. Chop the cabbage, potatoes, carrots, onions and parsley/parsnip into thin strips and add to the crispy bacon. Put all of this into a pan of boiling beef stock, then simmer until ready. Sprinkle with green herbs, salt and pepper. Traditionally served in clay pots.

Tsarskiye Shchi

---

[42] 'Shchi' traditionally refers to a variety of soups. The recipe offered presents one possibility.

Kasha to serve with the Shchi

Ingredients:
450 g (2⅔ cups) buckwheat
35 g (1¼ oz) butter
1–2 onions, chopped
3–4 mushrooms‡, finely chopped
120 ml (½ cup) mushroom stock
Wheat breadcrumbs to garnish
50–70 ml (4 tbsp) vegetable oil, plus extra for frying

Cooking method:
Preheat oven to 150 °C / 300 °F.

Add the butter to the buckwheat and cook over moderate heat until it turns a pinkish colour. Then place the fried grain into double its volume of boiling water, cover with a lid and place in the oven for 1 hour.

When the kasha is cooked, add 1–2 onions that have been fried in vegetable oil. Add the chopped mushrooms, along with the mushroom stock. Bring to the boil and stir. Place everything into a casserole dish and level the top of the kasha with a knife. Sprinkle with dried breadcrumbs and pour the vegetable oil over the top. Place in the oven for 5–10 minutes to allow the breadcrumbs to brown.

Traditionally, the kasha would be served on a side plate and eaten as an accompaniment to the shchi.

Kasha to serve with the Shchi

Cold Consommé

Recipe 1
(serves 5 or 6)

Ingredients:
500 g (13 cups) beetroot tops (beet greens)
100 g (3 cups) sorrel
100 g (¼ lb) boiled ox (beef) tongue
2 cucumbers
10 g (1½ tbsp) spring onions‡
100 g (¾ cup) radishes
2 hard-boiled eggs
10 g (1 cup) fresh dill and parsley
125 ml (½ cup) sour cream‡
Salt to taste

Cooking method:
Finely chop the beetroot tops, cover with boiling water and bring back to the boil. Add finely chopped sorrel and continue to boil for another 5 minutes. Add salt to taste and leave to cool until the stock is cold. Do not remove the beetroot or sorrel.

Finely chop the tongue, cucumbers, spring onion and radishes. Add to the cold stock.

When serving, add finely chopped egg and 1 tablespoon of sour cream per serving. Sprinkle with dill and parsley.

Okroshka with meat

Okroshka **with Meat**
A chilled Russian soup
(serves 5 or 6)

Ingredients:
220 g (½ lb) beef (silverside)
140 g (¼ lb) ox (beef) tongue
120 g (¾ cups) spring onions‡
Salt to taste
250 g (2 cups) cucumber
160 g (1 cup) piece of ham from the bone
4 hard-boiled eggs
20 g (5 tsp) granulated sugar‡
8 g (1½ tsp) English mustard
40 ml (2½ tbsp) sour cream‡ plus extra for serving
1.5 litres (1½ quarts) kvass (see p.95)
100 g (10 cups) fresh dill
2 potatoes, boiled and cubed

Cooking method:
Boil the silverside beef and ox tongue until cooked. Leave to cool and cut into small cubes.

Finely chop half the spring onions and then rub with salt. Then cut the cucumbers into cubes. (Outdoor cucumbers should be peeled but those cucumbers grown in greenhouses are best used with their skins on.) Cut the ham into cubes.

Reserving one egg for serving, separate the yolks from the whites of the remaining 3 eggs. Finely chop the egg whites.

For the okroshka liquid mash the egg yolks, salt, sugar, mustard and sour cream and the salted spring onions. Add the kvass and place in the fridge.

Mix the finely chopped meat, tongue, ham, remaining spring onions, egg yolks, cucumbers and egg whites. Then pour the chilled okroshka on top.

When serving, pour the okroshka into separate soup bowls, garnish each with a wedge of hard-boiled egg and sour cream. Sprinkle with fresh dill. Add boiled and cubed potatoes as an optional extra. Okroshka should be served at a temperature of 14–16 °C / 57–61 °F.

Pirozhki for Soup (without yeast)
(for 10–12 small pies)

Ingredients:
450 g (3½ cups) flour‡
150–170 ml (⅔–¾ cup) ice-cold water
280 g (10 oz) butter (cut into thin slices and kept at room temperature for recipe 1, or cubed and kept in a refrigerator for recipe 2)
1 egg
1 egg yolk
½ tsp salt
1 tbsp white vinegar

Cooking method:

Recipe 1
Sieve the flour and set it aside in a mixing bowl. Mix the white vinegar, egg, salt and water into the flour to make a pastry consistency. Roll the pastry out into a thin rectangular sheet and place the butter slices that have been kept at room temperature onto the central third of the sheet. Fold the longest edges of the pastry in to cover the central part from each side. Now fold in from each of the long ends to form a square shaped pastry filled with butter. Leave the pastry in a cool, dry place for one hour.

Next, roll the pastry out again to form one rectangular sheet and fold the pastry in the same way as before and roll out again into a rectangle. Repeat the folding, roll out again, repeat the folding once more and toll out again to the sheet from which you will cut the pirozhki circles.

Prepare the stuffing with any of the following: liver, beef, crayfish necks, fish, cabbage, carrots, rice potatoes or mushrooms. The instructions below are the same as the pirozhki with yeast (see p. 58) but you can adapt the number of sections to suit the quantity of pirozhki required.

To fill the pirozhki place some filling in the centre of each circle, then carefully join the edges together using a pinching motion to create the desired shape. It is important that the pinched edges are thick enough to ensure that no filling escapes during the baking process.

Preheat the oven to 210–220 °C / 410–430 °F . Place the filled pirozhki onto a greased baking tray with the pinched joints facing downwards and leave to rest for 10-15 minutes.

Pierce the pirozhki gently with a fork and brush with egg yolk; this seals their surfaces and will give them a lovely finished glaze.

Place in the oven until beautifully browned and crisp (approximately 20 minutes).

94

Serve them as a nice side dish to any clear soup.

Recipe 2 (easy version)

Sieve the flour and set it aside. Add the cubed butter to the flour and then blend the mixture with your fingers. Make a well in the centre of the flour and butter mixture. Pour in the ice-cold water, vinegar, egg and salt. Knead the pastry, then shape it into a ball, cover with a cloth and leave in a cold place for one hour. Roll it out and cut the dough into circles ready for making the pirozhki.

The rest is the same as recipe 1

Kvass

Ingredients:

400 g (4 cups) rye bread cut into croutons
15 g (5 tsp) fresh yeast (or 1 tsp fast-acting dry yeast)
300 g (1½ cups) granulated sugar‡
12 litres (3 gallons) water

Cooking method:

Dry fry the croutons, crumble them and stir gradually into 7 litres (7 quarts) of boiled water, cooled to 80 °C / 175 °F). Leave it to stand for 1 to 1½ hours in a warm place.

Strain off the liquid and reserve. Now cover the croutons with the remaining 5 litres (5 quarts) of hot water and leave for another 1 to 1½ hours in a warm place.

Dilute the yeast with a little warm water. Mix both strained liquids together, then add sugar and diluted yeast and leave it to brew for 8 to 12 hours at 25 °C / 75 °F.

Cool the kvass, pour into bottles, seal tightly with lids and keep at a temperature of no more than 10 °C / 50 °F.

Add mint, currants, juniper or thyme to taste before serving.

Quail with Red Cabbage

Recipe 1
(serves 5)

Ingredients:
10 quail

For marinade:
1 large onion, chopped
10 black peppercorns
2 bay leaves
50 g (¼ cup) granulated sugar‡
Salt to taste
200 ml (¾ cup) white vinegar
200 ml (¾ cup) red wine
250 ml (1 cup) water

1 red cabbage, chopped, boiled and marinated
Lettuce leaves
100 g (3½ oz) butter for frying

Cooking method:
Boil the chopped onion, pepper and bay leaves. Add the sugar and salt to taste. Remove from the heat. Add the vinegar and the wine before covering with a lid and leaving to cool.

In a large pan, fry the quail in butter for 10 minutes until they are cooked and leave to cool. Pour the marinade over the cooked quail. Place in a large jar, cover with a lid and put in a cool, dry place for 2–3 days.

If marinated cabbage is to be used, it should be prepared a day before serving. The boiled cabbage should be covered by equal amounts of water and vinegar, with sugar added to taste.

When ready to serve, remove the quail from the marinade, straining well. Any remaining, excess moisture can be removed with kitchen roll (paper towels). Place them on lettuce leaves alongside the boiled red cabbage.

Recipe 2
(serves 3 to 4)

<u>Ingredients:</u>
10 quail
100 g (3½ oz) butter for frying
10 black peppercorns
1 red cabbage
300 g (1⅓ cups) speck‡, cubed

<u>Cooking method:</u>
Preheat oven to 180 °C / 350 °F.
First prepare the quail, by soaking them in water with the peppercorns. Then place the birds in a deep pan. Fry them in the butter on all sides until the skin turns pinkish.
Place the quail in the oven for 10 to 15 minutes, basting from time to time with the butter, in which they were fried. When ready, place on top of the red cabbage (see below) in a warmed dish. Cover with pieces of fried speck and pour over the cooking juices.

Red cabbage to serve with Quail Recipe 2
(serves 3 to 4)

<u>Ingredients:</u>
2 onions, chopped
200 g (1 cup) cubed bacon‡
Flour‡
1 tbsp butter
1 red cabbage, chopped
Salt and pepper to taste
100 ml (½ cup) red wine

<u>Cooking method:</u>
Gently fry the onions and bacon in a frying pan with the butter. Sprinkle with flour and continue frying until golden. Mix with the chopped cabbage, season and bake for 30 minutes at 180 °C / 350 °F. Bring the wine to the boil and pour over the cabbage. Continue baking in the oven for a further 10–15 minutes.

Turkey Bake
(serves 4)[43]

Ingredients:
350 g (2¾ cups) turkey steaks cut into strips
140 g (1 cup) ham from the bone or gammon cut into strips
175 g (1¼ cups) frozen peas
50 g (3½ tbsp) butter
600 ml (2½ cups) milk‡
125 g (1 cup) flour‡
75 ml (½ cup) sherry
50 g (3 tbsp) Dijon type wholegrain mustard
Salt and pepper to taste
100 g (1 cup) grated cheddar cheese
50 g (½ cup) various chopped nuts (hazelnuts, almonds or walnuts)

This is an excellent dish for using up leftovers of any meat.

Cooking method:
Preheat the oven to 200 °C / 390 °F.

Mix the turkey, ham and frozen peas in an ovenproof dish.

Make the sauce by combining the butter, milk and flour in a saucepan. Bring it to the boil, whisking constantly until the sauce thickens. Add sherry, mustard and seasoning and sauté for 1 minute. Take off the heat and add half the cheese.

Cover the meat and peas with this sauce. Mix the remaining cheese with the nuts and sprinkle over the dish. At this point the prepared dish can be put in the fridge and kept for up to five hours before cooking or it can be frozen for a later date.

Bake in the oven for 25 to 35 minutes until golden.

---

[43] A contemporary recipe for roast turkey was unforthcoming. The above, however, is now a traditional method. The exact recipe for the roast turkey could not be found and it has been replaced with a turkey bake.

Quail with red cabbage

Strawberry and Champagne Jelly

Strawberry and Champagne Jelly
(serves 4)

Ingredients:
250 g (1¼ cups) strawberries
20 g (5 tsp) caster sugar‡
6 leaves white gelatine
Juice of 1 lemon
250 ml (1 cup) champagne
125 ml (½ cup) double cream, whipped‡

Cooking method:
Wash and hull the strawberries. Chop them, cover with caster sugar and leave for 30 minutes to allow the sugar to be absorbed. Place the gelatine in cold water for 10 minutes, strain and then melt in a saucepan over low heat, stirring continuously.

Slowly add the champagne, stirring until the jelly starts to thicken slightly. Remove from the heat and add the sugared strawberries. Stir again. Allow to cool slightly, then pour into dessert glasses and place in the fridge until set. When ready to serve, top with whipped double cream.

Strawberries with Champagne and Ice Cream
(serves 1)

Ingredients:
80 g (½ cup) strawberries
2 plain biscuits‡
70 ml (⅓ cup) champagne
100 g (⅔ cup) plombir[44] or vanilla ice cream

Preparation method:
Break up the biscuits and place in an appropriate dish. It should ideally then be one third full.

Place the cleaned and chilled strawberries on top of the biscuit. If the strawberries are too large, simply cut them in half.

Cover with champagne and add balls of ice cream. Serve immediately.

---

[44] deriving from French plombières (made with almond extract, kirsch and candied fruit), this uses sweet condensed milk and is creamier than western ice cream

Riz à l'Impératrice[45]
(serves 6)

Ingredients:
125 g (⅔ cup) rice
750 ml (3 cups) milk‡
100 g (½ cup) granulated sugar‡
Pinch of salt
30 g (1 oz) butter
1 vanilla pod, cut in half and deseeded
100–125 g (⅔ cup) apricot purée or dried apricots
60 g (⅓ cup) fruit mixture (grapes, cherries, pieces of pineapple, and pieces of angelica) soaked in 100 ml (½ cup) Kirsch or cherry vodka with 25 g (¼ cups) icing sugar‡
500 ml (2 cups) scalded cream‡ with 1 tsp dissolved gelatine
75 ml (⅓ cup) Kirsch

Cooking method:
Preheat the oven to 150 °C / 300 °F.

Parboil the rice in boiling water for 5 minutes. Strain, cool in cold water and drain. Place the rice in a casserole dish or a deep saucepan; add boiling milk, sugar, a pinch of salt, butter and vanilla. Cover with a tight lid, put into the oven and cook for 30 minutes or until the liquid has been fully absorbed.

Remove the vanilla pod, mix the rice with the apricot purée or coarsely chopped dried apricots and then add the fruit mixture. Cover everything with scalded cream containing the gelatine and Kirsch, and place the rice mixture into a dish greased with butter. Place in the fridge for 4–5 hours before serving.

---

[45] The phrase "à l'Impératrice" (Empress style) derives from Eugénie de Montijo, who as the spouse of Napoleon III became the last Empress of France in August 1870. It tends to refer to sweet or savoury rice-based dishes, whereas "à l'Impériale" (Imperial style: see e.g. Sterlet à l'Impériale on page 104 or the jellied version on page 157) covers rich dishes such as salmon or trout garnished with crayfish tails, truffles, cocks' combs, kidneys or foie gras. However, one can also find references to "Imperial Rice Pudding (Pouding de Riz à l'Impériale)" describing a sweet dish very similar to the female version: for example, Joseph Favre's famous Dictionnaire universel de cuisine pratique includes both, q.v.
https://gallica.bnf.fr/ark:/12148/bpt6k57300438/f345.image

DEJEUNER
du 5 Octobre 1913.

Potage-Crême de Crevettes
Consommé St Hubert
Petits pâtés
Sterlets à l'Impériale
Poulardes du Mans Argenteuil
S-ce Ivoire
Pain de Faisans Victoria
S-ce Chutney
Salade pommes de terre et
truffes
Gâteau Marquise
Ananas à la Parisienne
Dessert.

Original French menu

5 OCTOBER 1913

Dinner

Creamed Prawn Soup
Consommé 'St Hubert'[46]
Pirozhki
Sterlet à l'Impériale
Poulardes Argenteuil
Ivory sauce
Pheasant bake 'Victoria'
Chutney sauce
Potato and truffle salad
Gateau 'Marquise'
Pineapple à la Parisienne

From this day in Russian history:

> *The weather is a little warmer now. In the morning Alexei received presents in our bedroom. I went for a walk. At 11 am there was a church parade in front of the house for all the units from the Yalta garrison, following which there was a ceremony for the promotion of navel cadets. In the dining hall about 160 people had breakfast. Alexei and I then took part in a group photo. At 2 pm, by which time everybody had finished talking, we changed and went to play tennis. Later on we received Grigori who stayed until 7.45 pm. There then followed a magnificent display of fireworks presented by the navy, whose ships were at anchor in the harbour. Against a background of a calm sea and a full moon this was indeed a splendid show. To enjoy the spectacle even more, we went down to Yalta, to the Embankment.*
>
> *From the Diary of Nicholas II*

ೞ

On 5 October, which was the Name Day of the Tsarevich, the Grand Duke Alexei Nikolayevich, there was an army parade of units based near Yalta ...

> *At 11 am the Emperor left the Palace in full uniform and wearing the order of St Andrew. After receiving a report from the Parade*

---

[46] This is what is shown in the original (French) menu, but is surely a mistake, as 'St Hubert' normally refers to a thick game soup. We have therefore included recipes for both game soup and consommé.

Commander, Major General Dumbadze, the Imperial Entourage, led by the Grand Dukes Dmitri Konstantinovich, Pyotr Nikolayevich, Georgi Mikhailovich, Alexander Mikhailovich and Prince Sergey Georgievich Romanovsky, inspected the troops. The air resounded with cheers and the sound of the Imperial Anthem".

At the same time, a special service of prayers took place in the presence of the Empress Alexandra Feodorovna, accompanied by the Tsesarevich[47], who was dressed in military uniform and wearing the order of St Andrew. The Imperial Daughters were also present. At the end of the service, at the point when the words 'God grant you many years' were sung in honour of the Imperial Family, a salute was fired from the ships of the Black Sea Navy.

Nicholas II then addressed a parade of officers and men of the Black Sea Navy and special Imperial congratulations were offered to those who had received promotion.

Following this, a celebratory meal was served in the main dining hall of the Livadia Palace. The Imperial Family was joined by a most impressive array of guests, including not only the highest aristocracy but also many military, naval and other dignitaries. These lists of guests were reported in considerable detail as the following, fascinating extract shows:

"The guests included their Imperial Highnesses and their children; Grand Dukes who had been present at the Parade; His Highness the Emir of Bukhara; Grand Duchess Militsa Nikolayevna, Princesses Tatyana Konstantinovna, Marina Petrovna, Anna Alexandrovna and Yelena Georgievna Romanovskaya; Prince Nikita Alexandrovich.

Also present were Imperial Minister Count Freedericksz and his wife who was lady-in-waiting to the Empress; ladies-in-waiting to the Imperial Court; various Imperial Maids of Honour. To all these people were added many navy and military dignitaries and other visitors, including the local Police Chief. During the meal everyone was entertained by the Choir of the Tsarevich's 51st Lithuanian Infantry."

Russian Riviera, 7 October 1913

ೞಬಿ

---

[47] Heir Apparent – a title distinct from *Tsarevich* (meaning simply "Tsar's son")

On 8 October 1913 *Russian Riviera* reported amongst other stories:

A new venture on the estate of the Princes Trubetskoy near Alupka. This venture was the construction of a poultry farm for supplying the tables of titled nobility, with any surplus being sold in the local market.

A recent storm had swept a bronze statue of a mermaid away from the estate of Prince Yusupov. No trace of it had been found during subsequent searches.

A new Slavic Society had been inaugurated in Moscow to introduce to the people of Russia all matters of general Slavonic interest.

CAEO

Empress Alexandra Feodorovna with Tsarevich Alexei, 1913.
From the photographic archives of the Livadia Palace Museum.

Prawn Soup

Recipe 1
(serves 8)

Ingredients:
1 onion, finely chopped
1 carrot, peeled and finely chopped
1 bulb celeriac‡, peeled and finely chopped
30 g (1 oz) butter
500 g (5 cups) prawns‡, shelled[48]
1.5 l (1½ quarts) water
100 g (1 cup) large prawns‡, unshelled
80 g (⅔ cup) mushrooms‡, boiled and cut into thin strips
50 g (⅓ cup) flour‡
180 ml (¾ cup) buttermilk‡
2 eggs
Fresh green herbs
Salt to taste
Pepper to taste
1 tbsp of butter
1 lemon

Cooking method:
Lightly fry the onion, carrot and celeriac in butter. Wash the prawns and add to the vegetables. Mix together and place in a saucepan. Add the water and simmer for 25–30 minutes. Remove the prawns and squeeze out their juices.

Simmer the unshelled large prawns separately. Discard the shells and reserve the prawns to use as a garnish for the soup.

Now, add the boiled mushrooms to the soup, stir the flour into the buttermilk and add it together with the beaten eggs. Sprinkle with finely chopped fresh green herbs and add the seasoning. Finally, add butter and the lemon juice and top with large prawns. Serve hot.

---

[48] To avoid any possible confusion: shelled = with shells removed, unshelled = with shells still attached.

Recipe 2
(serves 8)

<u>Ingredients:</u>
900 g (2 lb) beef shank
200 g (½ lb) veal bones
1 bunch parsley
3 celery‡ ribs
3 trimmed leeks
4 carrots, peeled
1 onion, peeled
1.5 l (1½ quarts) water

200–300 g (2–3 cups) prawns‡
1 parsnip
2 carrots, peeled
1 onion, peeled
1 nutmeg, grated
25 g (1 oz) butter
12 g (1½ tbsp) flour‡
100 ml (½ cup) sour cream‡ or single cream‡
Fresh dill to serve

<u>Cooking method:</u>
Make the stock by simmering the beef, veal bones, parsley, celery, leeks, 2 carrots and 1 onion in the water.

Boil the prawns for 3–4 minutes. Peel, then chop into small pieces. Remove the vegetables from the stock and finely chop.

Boil the other 2 carrots, parsnip, 1 onion and nutmeg together until soft. Liquidize in a food processor with the butter. Place this mixture in a frying pan, along with the flour and then fry for a few minutes. Add the sour cream or single cream and stock and bring to the boil. Simmer for 5 minutes. To serve, add the chopped prawns and fresh dill.

Prawn Soup

Cream of Game Soup 'St Hubert'
(serves 10)

Ingredients:
500 g (2½ cups) brown lentils, soaked
1 onion, finely chopped
1 leek, well-trimmed and finely chopped
Pinch of thyme or dill
1 bay leaf
2 tsp salt
1 pheasant or blackcock (black grouse), or
3 grey partridges, or
4 white partridges, all plucked and cleaned
180 ml (¾ cup) single cream‡

Cooking method:
Place the soaked lentils in a saucepan, along with the onion, leek, thyme or dill and bay leaf. Cover with water, add salt and simmer until the lentils are soft.

Fry the game and then simmer in water until cooked. When the game is ready, separate the meat from the bones. Place the carcass back into the prepared stock and simmer for another 20–30 minutes.

Select the best pieces of game and liquidize the rest of the meat in a food processor. Add the lentils and process once again. Add some stock to the mixture before returning it to the pan and heating. Gradually add the rest of the stock, stirring continuously to obtain a smooth consistency. Slowly add the cream, continuing to stir. Season with salt and heat through once again.

Before serving, cut the reserved meat into thin strips to serve as garnish.

Consommé with Vegetables and Egg à la Parisienne
(serves 8)

Ingredients:
160 g (2½ cups) carrots, peeled
60 g (⅔ cup) celery‡
160 g (1 cup) whole green beans‡
160 g (1 cup) mangetout‡
180 g (½ cup) cauliflower
4 litres (1 gallon) prepared vegetable stock
8 eggs, poached
80 g (⅔ cup) chopped parsley
Salt and pepper to taste

Cooking method:
Chop the cleaned carrots, celery, green beans and mangetout into small cubes. Separate the cauliflower into small florets. Simmer all the vegetables in the stock until cooked. Place a poached egg in each serving bowl. Add some vegetables and cover with stock. Season and garnish with finely chopped parsley.

Sterlet à l'Impériale
(12 vol-au-vents cases)

Ingredients:
800 g (3–4 cups) skinned sterlet[‡] to fill 12 *vol-au-vents cases*
100 ml (½ cup) dry white wine
salt to taste
1 onion, finely chopped
300 g (1⅓ cups) mayonnaise
1 tsp Worcestershire sauce
1 tsp parsley, chopped
1 tsp ground black pepper
Grated rind of 1 lemon
12 vol-au-vents
1 sweet pepper[‡]

Cooking method:
Cut the sterlet into large pieces, and cover with the wine and salt. Simmer gently for 10 minutes. Add the onion and continue to cook for another 10 minutes. Allow to cool and then cut the fish into large cubes. Mix with the mayonnaise, Worcestershire sauce, chopped parsley, ground black pepper and grated lemon rind. Fill the vol-au-vents with the prepared mixture, and then decorate with thin slices of lemon and sweet pepper.

Worcestershire Sauce

Recipe 1

One tenth of this sauce is tomato paste, with the remaining nine tenths containing 25 ingredients. Unlike many other tomato-based sauces, the taste of tomato is not overpowering but works perfectly with the other flavours.

To achieve a perfect balance, a large batch of sauce is prepared – 10 kg – and for this the following ingredients are required:

Ingredients:
950 g (4 cups) tomato paste
190 ml (1 cup) ready-made black walnut extract
570 ml (2½ cups) mushroom stock
80 g (11 tbsp) ground black pepper
760 ml (3 cups) dessert wine such as Tokai
570 g (2½ cups) tamarind
190 g (8 tbsp) anchovies
100 g (1 cup) curry powder
340 g (2½ cups) cayenne pepper
4 g (2 tsp) allspice
190 g (¾ cup) lemon, finely chopped
40 g (2⅔ tbsp) horseradish
80 g (⅔ cup) celery‡
80 g (5 tbsp) meat extract
70 g (½ cup) aspic
2.3 litres (2¼ quarts) malt vinegar
3 litres (3 quarts) water
1 g (½ tsp)[49] ground ginger
1 g (½ tsp) bay leaf
4 g (2 tsp) ground nutmeg
230 g (¾ cup) salt
1 g (¼ tsp) chilli pods
18 g (1 tbsp) caramel
10 g (2 tsp) tarragon vinegar

---

[49] Although the 1 g spices result in a concentration of just 0.01% (100 ppm), they may add a 'homeopathic' contribution to the final taste!

Cooking method:

Combine all the ingredients in an extra-large, heavy pot. Bring to the boil and simmer, stirring occasionally until the sauce has thickened and will coat the back of a spoon.

Strain into glass bottles and refrigerate.

Recipe 2

Ingredients:

5 litre (1 gallon) glass jar
1 tin red kidney beans in salted water
1 bottle soy sauce
1 tsp garlic powder (or 2 crushed cloves fresh garlic)
2 tins sardines in oil
1.6 l (1⅔ quarts) red wine vinegar
5 kg (11 lb) green apples, peeled and chopped
1 onion, chopped
75 g (⅔ cup) ground cloves
50 g (⅓ cup) ground turmeric
50 g (½ cup) ground nutmeg
50 g (½ cup) ground black pepper
50 g (½ cup) instant coffee powder
2 tsp paprika
100 ml (½ cup) golden syrup or any thick sugar syrup
125 g (½ cup) salt
75 g (¼ cup) English mustard powder
25 g (¼ cup) sugar‡

Cooking method:

Empty the tin of red kidney beans into a sieve and drain, wash the beans and crush into a purée. Place the purée into a glass jar, add the soy sauce and garlic.

Place the sardines into a metal bowl, mash into a purée and add a splash of vinegar, then add this mixture to the kidney bean purée.

Put the chopped apples into a saucepan and cover them with vinegar. Add the onion, ground cloves, turmeric, nutmeg, pepper and coffee. Bring to the boil and simmer, without a lid, over a low heat for 2 hours. As the vinegar evaporates, add water and vinegar in equal amounts, making sure the apples are covered by liquid at all times.

Stir it from time to time, as the apples tend to stick to the bottom of the pan and might burn.

113

After 2 hours, take the saucepan off the heat, liquidize the mixture until puréed and add 8 cups of the purée to the jar. Add the paprika, syrup, salt, mustard and sugar. If the jar is not filled to the top, add some vinegar. Mix it thoroughly by shaking the jar and leave in a cool place for 24 hours. Then drain the mixture and pour into bottles with secure tops.

Vol-au-vents

Vol-au-vents can, of course, be bought ready-made. If, however, you wish to make your own, this can be done most effectively using sheets of ready-made puff pastry. If you decide to do this yourself, cut out as many rounds as possible from the pastry. A coffee can or large wine glass would produce an ideal size. Place half of the rounds on a baking tray. Cut out the middle part from the remaining rounds and place the rounds on the bases already on the baking tray. Use up all the rounds. Grease with egg yolk and bake in an oven at 250–260 °C / 480–500 °F for 25–30 minutes. Leave to cool and fill the vol-au-vents with fillings to taste.

Rooster or Poularde Argenteuil
(serves 4)

Ingredients:
1.5 kg (3⅓ lb) whole rooster or poularde‡
30 g (¼ cup) onions, finely chopped
30 g (½ cup) carrots, peeled and finely chopped
30 g (¼ cup) celery‡, finely chopped
Salt to taste
75 g (⅔ cup) flour‡
120 g (4¼ oz) butter
200 ml (1 cup) double cream‡
2 egg yolks
Juice of 1 lemon
1 kg (4 cups) white asparagus
300 g (2 cups) green peas
Cos lettuce‡ to serve

Cooking method:
Cover the bird with cold water, bring to the boil and remove any froth. Add the onion, carrot, celery and salt and simmer on a low heat until cooked. Remove the bird and put the stock aside. Brown the flour in the butter to make a roux. Dilute with around 1 cup of the stock, stirring constantly, and then gradually add the cream, continuing to stir. Season.

Remove the sauce from the heat. Add the lemon juice and beaten egg yolks. Then strain. Cut the cooked bird into serving portions, place on a large dish and pour the sauce over it. Garnish with cooked asparagus, green peas softened in butter and lettuce leaves.

Sauce Parisienne

Ingredients:
100–125 ml (½ cup) freshly cooked mushroom sauce
600 ml (2½ cups) clear chicken stock
5 egg yolks
Pinch of coarsely ground black pepper
1 medium-sized nutmeg, grated
1.2 l (5 cups) white sauce
A little clarified butter

Cooking method:

Mushroom Sauce
1 tsp butter
75 g (1 cup) sliced mushrooms‡
75 ml (5 tbsp) double cream‡
½ tsp ground black pepper
½ tsp ground sea salt

Heat the butter over moderate heat. Add the mushrooms and stir-fry until lightly browned. Reduce heat and add cream and seasoning. Simmer, stirring constantly, for 5–8 minutes until the sauce has reduced by half.

Chicken Stock
2 kg (4½ lbs) chicken bones and giblets
2 onions, chopped
1 leek, washed and chopped
3 celery‡ ribs chopped
1 bay leaf
Sprigs of thyme
10 black peppercorns

Chop the chicken bones with a cleaver and then wash thoroughly in cold water. Place in a saucepan, cover with cold water and bring to the boil. Turn down the heat and simmer gently for 90 minutes, skimming the froth from time to time. Strain the stock through a fine meshed sieve.

White Sauce
1 litre (1 quart) milk‡
20 black peppercorns
2 slices onion
2 bay leaves
2 blades mace (or 1 tsp ground mace)
Parsley stalks, chopped
50 g (¼ cup) flour‡
100 g (3½ oz) butter

Place the milk and the seasonings in a heavy pan. Slowly bring the milk to a simmer. Then remove from the heat and allow to cool completely.

Strain to remove the flavourings, then add the flour and butter. Slowly bring back to the boil, whisking vigorously to keep the sauce smooth. Cook gently for 5 minutes to allow the sauce to thicken.

Sauce Parisienne
Mix the mushroom sauce, clear stock, egg yolks, pepper and nutmeg together in a heavy saucepan. While whisking the mixture, add the white sauce and bring to the boil. Cook rapidly until the mixture has attained the consistency of a thick sauce. Strain though a fine sieve. Stir it slightly and cover with a thin layer of melted clarified butter to prevent a skin forming. Store until required.

Pheasant Bake 'Victoria'
(for 1 pheasant)

Ingredients:
1 pheasant, plucked and cleaned
80 g (⅓ cup) speck‡
Salt
140 g (5 oz) butter
5 large onions, chopped
6 black peppercorns
500 g (3⅔ cups) fried rice
Ground nutmeg to taste
50 g (2 cups) parsley and spring onions‡, chopped
Splash of milk

Béchamel sauce:
30 g (¼ cup) flour‡
50 g (2 oz) butter

Cooking method:
Wash the pheasant, and then stuff it with speck keeping back a few pieces. Rub it with salt. Melt the butter in a frying pan. Add chopped onions, the remaining pieces of speck and black peppercorns. Add the pheasant and fry until cooked. Remove the pheasant and leave to cool. Separate the meat from the bones and chop into small pieces. Mix with the fried onions.

Cook the rice, then cool it and fry in a little oil.

Béchamel sauce:
Melt the butter. Add the flour and stir to make a roux. Then add the juices from frying the pheasant and a splash of milk, and continue stirring to make a lovely, thick sauce. If necessary, add a little extra water. Stir the pheasant meat into the sauce, add fried rice and salt and nutmeg to taste. Place the mixture in a buttered dish, cover the top with thin layers of butter and bake quickly. Serve the dish warm or cold with sprinkled parsley and spring onions and a light salad of lettuce and tomatoes.

Chutney Sauce

Ingredients:
200 g (1⅓ cups) figs
200 g (1⅓ cups) gooseberries
2 chillies
1 clove garlic
25 g (8 tsp) garam masala
250 ml (1 cup) rice wine vinegar

Cooking method:
Deseed the figs and put them in a metal bowl together with the gooseberries. Clean, deseed and chop the chillies and add to the fruit. Now add the crushed garlic, garam masala and vinegar. Sauté gently until the chutney has the consistency of porridge.

Potatoes Stuffed with Mushrooms

Recipe 1
(serves 10)

Ingredients:
5 medium potatoes
1 onion, chopped
1 tsp margarine
250 g (2⅔ cups) mushrooms‡, sliced
30 ml (2 tbsp) white wine
2 vegetable stock cubes‡
200 ml (1 cup) single cream‡
150 g (1½ cups) grated Cheddar type cheese

Cooking method:
Preheat the oven to 150 °C / 300 °F.

Cut the potatoes lengthwise into two halves. Scoop out the middle of each with a spoon to obtain the shape of a small boat. Place the potato boats in 1 litre of boiling salted water and boil for 5 minutes. Now put these onto a baking tray and fill them with the prepared stuffing. Sprinkle the grated cheese on top and bake for 20 minutes.

Stuffing:
Fry the onion in margarine, add the sliced mushrooms, wine and stock cubes and mix together. Pour in the cream and bring to the boil. Cook on a low heat until it thickens (about 8–10 minutes).

Recipe 2

Ingredients:
5 medium potatoes
500 g (4 cups) mushrooms of choice
Sunflower/corn oil for frying
1 large onion, chopped
2 cloves garlic, crushed
100 ml (½ cup) white wine
500 ml (2¼ cups) double cream‡
100 g (¾ cup) nuts (pine nuts might be particularly suitable)
Salt and pepper to taste
150 g (1½ cups) mature Cheddar type cheese, grated

Cooking method:
Preheat the oven to 150 °C / 300 °F.

Peel the potatoes and cut them lengthwise into two halves. Scoop out the middle part and boil these potato boats in salted water until almost cooked. Now place these on a baking tray face upwards.

Chop the mushrooms, add the chopped onion and fry together in the oil on a high heat for 15–20 minutes, stirring occasionally. Reduce the heat. Add wine, cream, nuts, salt and a little pepper. Sauté without a lid for 10–15 minutes, stirring gently. In the final 5 minutes, add half the cheese. Spoon the stuffing into the potatoes until well filled and then sprinkle on the remaining cheese. Bake for 10 minutes and serve piping hot.

Jam Tart baked 'à la Marquise'

Ingredients:
200–250 g (1 cup) margarine, slightly melted and softened
100 g (½ cup) granulated sugar‡
½ tsp baking soda, mixed with a little white vinegar
600 g (4 cups) flour‡
2 eggs
Fruit jam‡ or sautéed apples

Cooking method:
Preheat the oven to 160 °C / 320 °F.

Rub the margarine into the dry ingredients. Bind the mixture with the eggs, mixing thoroughly until the mixture is smooth. Halve the mixture. Form several balls from one half and place them in the freezer for 30–40 minutes until firm. Roll the other half of the mixture and place on a baking tray. Crimp the edges. Spread the jam or apples on top. If using apples, these should have been sautéed lightly in butter and flavoured with sugar, cinnamon and vanilla. Remove the balls from the freezer. They should be firm enough to be minced (ground) or coarsely grated and sprinkled evenly over the filling. Bake until cooked and cut into pieces while still hot.

Pineapples in Champagne
(serves 2)

Ingredients:
320 ml (1⅓ cups) sugar syrup (see below)
40 ml (2⅔ tbsp) pineapple or mango juice
2 pineapple slices, chopped
100 ml (½ cup) champagne or white wine
Ice

Mix all the ingredients together, then pour into champagne glasses.

Sugar syrup
250 ml (1 cup) water
500 g (2½ cups) caster sugar‡

Bring the water to the boil. Dissolve the sugar in the boiling water, stirring constantly. Remove the pan from the heat. Cool and then bottle. (Should you wish to prolong the shelf life of your syrup, add a tablespoon of vodka once it is cool.)

Déjeuner
du 22 Octobre 1913

Potage Faubonne
Petits pâtés
Coq de mer Italienne S.ᵗᵉ provençale
Oeufs en daube
Mouton chops pomme de terre Anna
Gélinottes à la crème aux gribouis
Tarte aux Mirabelles
Macédoine de fruits

Original French menu

124

22 OCTOBER 1913

Dinner

Soup 'Faubourne'
Pirozhki
Gurnard, Italian style
Sauce Provençale
Baked eggs
Mutton
Pommes 'Anna'
Grouse in sour cream
Mirabelle plum tart
Fruit Macédoine

From this day in Russian history:

Another wonderful day. Nicholasha came to see me in the morning. Attended the Liturgy and then had breakfast in the best Sunday tradition. Played tennis for a little while and then we all went for a walk together. We returned home for tea through Oreanda. Received Sukhomlinov before dinner. Read all evening and finished the papers.

From the diary of Nicholas II

෨★ల

Yesterday was indeed a very special day. It was the anniversary of the Accession to the Throne of our Sovereign Emperor. There were special ceremonial services and litanies in all the churches and cathedrals of Yalta and Livadia. A special service was also held in the Synagogue at Yalta and was conducted by Cantor Stasevich. During the day, the town was richly decorated with flags and fully illuminated in the evening.

෫8෨

The chrysanthemum show was opened on 20 October in one of the pavilions of the former agricultural exhibition. Visitors were treated to a rich display of the many varieties of chrysanthemums and enjoyed a scene of magnificent blossoms. Amongst the participants were the Natashino Estate, the town nursery and Mr Guriev's famous flower shop. The show will be running for a few more days yet. Starting from today, the entrance to the show is free.

Today, 22 October, in the Novikov Theatre, there will be a presentation of the Staritsky's comedy "A Bird in the Hand is worth Two in the Bush". The performance, given by the Ukrainian company of B. Orshanov and V. Danchenko, will commence at 8.30 pm There are four acts, all with singing and dancing.

Russian Riviera, 22 October 1913

Dinner on the yacht *Standart*. March 1912
From the photographic archives of the Livadia Palace Museum.

Old English Soup
(serves 4)

Recipe 1

The original old Russian recipe for Potage 'Faubourne' has unfortunately been lost. We suggest therefore two similar recipes, taken from old English cuisine

Ingredients:
1 chicken
350 g (2⅓ cups) boiled ham
1 onion, chopped
2 celery‡ ribs, sliced
3 carrots, sliced
Large pinch of thyme
Pinch of ground nutmeg
Salt and pepper to taste
3 egg yolks
120 ml (½ cup) double cream‡
6 g (1½ tbsp) parsley, chopped

Cooking method:
Cut the chicken into several parts and soak in cold, salted water for about 30 minutes. Rinse the pieces and place in a large saucepan, together with the ham, onion, celery, carrot and spices. Cover with water. Bring to the boil and remove any froth. Simmer for one hour. Remove the meat and mince (grind) it. Ensure all bones are removed and skim off any excess fat. Sieve or liquidize the soup. Pour it into a clean saucepan and bring it slowly back to the boil. Simmer for five minutes, and then add the chopped chicken meat.

Whisk the egg yolks and cream and add some hot stock to this mixture, before adding it to the soup. Stir for a few minutes but do not let it boil. To serve, garnish with parsley.

Recipe 2
(serves 4)

Ingredients:
1 onion
1 carrot
1 turnip
75 ml (⅓ cup) vegetable oil
½ tsp curry powder
6 black peppercorns
3–4 cloves
50 g (¼ cup) brown lentils
50 g (⅓ cup) currants
1.5 l (1½ quarts) beef or chicken stock

Cooking method:
Cut the onion, carrot and turnip into cubes. Fry them in vegetable oil until golden. Add the curry powder, peppercorns and cloves and continue frying for a further few minutes. Put everything into a saucepan, add the washed lentils and currants and cover with stock. Bring to the boil and simmer for 40 to 45 minutes. When you are ready to serve remove the cloves and peppercorns.

Gurnard
(serves 2)

Ingredients:
400 g (¾ lb) gurnard‡ (or other appropriate sea fish)
1 onion
1 parsnip
100 ml (½ cup) dry white wine
6 ripe tomatoes
1 clove garlic
100 ml (½ cup) olive oil
25 g (1¾ tbsp) tomato paste
350 g (3½ cups) penne pasta
Sprigs of parsley
Salt to taste

Cooking method:
Clean the fish thoroughly and fillet it. Wash and cut into small pieces. Reserve the fish head and bones for the stock.

Preparation of stock:
Peel the onion and cut into two halves. Peel and halve the parsnip. Place the onion, parsnip, fish heads and bones in a saucepan. Add the white wine and 200 ml (1 cup) of water. Bring the stock to the boil, reduce the heat, cover with a lid and simmer for at least 20 minutes. Strain the stock but keep it warm.

Preparation of sauce:
Peel the tomatoes after loosening the skins with boiling water. Chop the flesh. In a large frying pan sauté the peeled and chopped garlic in olive oil. Now add the tomatoes, tomato paste and the pieces of fish. Sauté for at least 10 minutes, occasionally turning the fish.

Boil the penne pasta in a large quantity of salted water. Just before the sauce is ready, drain the pasta and place in a frying pan with the fish stock and parsley. Season to taste. Stirring very carefully, cook gently until all the liquid has evaporated. Serve with the cooked fish and sauce.

Sauce Provençale for Fish

Ingredients:
2 hard-boiled egg yolks
1–2 tsp granulated sugar‡
1 tsp French mustard
Salt
200 ml (1 cup) vegetable oil
5–6 drops white vinegar
18 g (3¾ tbsp) tarragon or (3½ tsp) capers (optional)

Cooking method:
Mix the egg yolks, sugar, mustard, and a pinch of salt together until the mixture is thick and then add the vegetable oil and 5–6 drops of vinegar. At this point you may add the tarragon or capers (if using) and mix it all together.

Gurnard

Baked Eggs
(serves 4)

Ingredients:
8 slices white bread
200 g (7 oz) butter (you may need slightly more)
100 g (⅔ cup) smoked ham on the bone, sliced
8 eggs
Salt to taste
Pepper to taste
Small bunch spring onions[‡]

Cooking method:
Preheat oven to 180 °C / 350 °F.

Fry the bread slices in the butter. Grease a heatproof dish with the fat from the frying pan, arrange the toast on the bottom and put a thin slice of smoked ham on each slice. Beat the eggs thoroughly until they are of even consistency and then add salt and pepper. Add finely chopped spring onions. Cover the toast with the mixture and bake in the oven for 6 minutes.

Pommes 'Anna'
(serves 2)

Ingredients:
250 g (1⅔ cups) waxy potatoes, peeled and thinly sliced
Salt to taste
Ground black pepper to taste
15 g (1 tbsp) melted butter

Cooking method:
Preheat oven to 200 °C / 400 °F.

Rub the thin slices of peeled potatoes with salt and pepper and arrange in circles in several layers in a buttered ovenproof dish, sprinkling each layer with butter. Cover with a lid and put in a hot oven for 30 minutes. Then flip the potatoes over and place back in the oven for a further 5 minutes without the lid.

Grouse in Sour Cream
(serves 2)

Ingredients:
2 grouse
2 litres (2 quarts) cold milk‡
50–70 g (¼ cup) lardons (thick bacon‡)
Salt to taste
Pepper to taste
20 g (1½ tbsp) lard‡
180 ml (¾ cup) sour cream‡
2 waxy potatoes sliced
Fresh herbs

Cooking method:
If the grouse are bought from a shop and have been stored for some time, first pluck them and soak them in cold water for 2 hours. If the birds are fresh however, one hour of soaking will be enough. Place them in a saucepan, cover with cold milk and bring to the boil. Reserve 400 ml of the milk stock.

Now the grouse are ready for frying. Remove the head and wings. Leave the legs as they are, but remove the claws. Sear the grouse over a high heat. To increase flavour and juiciness, make small incisions and insert pieces of thick bacon. Cut the birds in half; add salt and pepper and fry in a saucepan with pork lard until crispy. Then add the reserved milk stock to the saucepan, cover with a lid and simmer on a low heat until fully cooked.

Add some juices from the frying pan to the sour cream and stir. Pour the sauce over the grouse and boil for 1–2 minutes. Fry the pieces of potatoes. Put the game bird on a serving dish and arrange the potato pieces around it. Pour some sour cream sauce all over and sprinkle with fresh herbs.

Mirabelle Plum Tart
(serves 6 to 8)

Ingredients:
800 g (4½ cups) Mirabelle (cherry) plums
150 g (⅔ cup) caster sugar‡
50 ml (¼ cup) plum vodka
20 g (⅔ oz) butter
1 round sheet of shortcrust pastry
40 g (⅓ cup) ground almonds
40 g (⅓ cup) ground pistachios
25 g (3⅓ tbsp) cornflour‡
3 eggs
250 ml (1 cup) single cream‡

Cooking method:
Preheat the oven to 210 °C / 410 °F.

Cut the plums in half and remove the stones. Place in a metal bowl, add sugar and pour in the vodka. Leave to marinate in a fridge for 1 hour.

Grease a baking dish with butter and place the pastry inside. Pierce the pastry with a fork and then turn up the edges. Mix the almonds and pistachio nuts together and sprinkle the base of the pastry with the nut mixture. Strain the plums and reserve the marinade. Arrange the plums on top of the pastry.

Stir the cornflour into the marinade juice. Add the eggs to the mixture and whisk while gradually adding the cream. Pour the mixture over the plums. Put the baking tray in the oven and bake for 35 minutes until the pastry turns golden and the plums become caramelized.

Take the baking dish out of the oven and leave to cool for 10 minutes. Remove the pie and place it on a serving dish. Serve when the pie is completely cool.

Mirabelle Plum Tart

Apricot, Cherry and Berry Macédoine
(serves 4)

Ingredients:
300 g (1⅓ cups) apricots
250 g (1 cup) cherries
200 g (1¼ cups) strawberries
200 g (2 cups) raspberries
1 kg (5 cups) caster sugar‡
200 g (2 cups) redcurrants

This dish needs to be prepared the day before. Stone the apricots and cherries and remove the stalks from the other fruit. Keep the berries and the other fruit separate. Gradually add separate layers of berries and fruit to a large glass jar and then cover with the sugar. Leave the jar at room temperature until all the sugar has fully dissolved and then refrigerate. Serve cold in crystal glasses.

Autumn Macédoine with Ice Cream
(serves 4)

Ingredients:
1 apple
1 pear
1 medium-sized bunch of grapes
100 g (½ cup) strawberries
100 g (½ cup) tinned apricots in syrup
100 g (½ cup) caster sugar‡
Juice of 1 lemon
4 scoops of vanilla ice cream

Cooking method:
Peel the apple and pear, remove the cores and cut into medium-sized cubes. Place the fruit in a metal bowl and pour half the lemon juice over. Remove the grapes from their stalks, wash and dry. Wash the strawberries, cut each in half lengthwise. Take the apricots out of their syrup, leave them to drain and cut them into thin slices. Place the fruit in a deep dish, sprinkle with sugar and the rest of the lemon juice. Carefully mix the fruit and separate the mixture into 4 glasses. Cover with cling-film and refrigerate for 30 minutes. Serve the macédoine with a scoop of ice cream in each glass.

Note: fruit macédoine can be served with any type of ice cream, except for chocolate or nut. These two flavours are too overpowering for the delicate flavours of the fruit.

DÉJEUNER
du 6 Décembre 1913.

Potages { Tortue à l'Anglaise
Crème Princesse

Petits pâtés

Stoudine de Sterlet à l'Impériale

Longe de Veau Moscovite

Poulardes du Mans truffées

S-ce Périgueu

Pêches Cardinal

Corbeille de glaces Parisienne

Dessert.

Original French menu

6 DECEMBER 1913

Breakfast

Soup 'à la Tortue'
Cream soup 'Princess'
Pirozhki
Jellied Sterlet à l'Impériale
Roast Veal Moscow style
Poulardes stuffed with Truffles
Sauce Périgueux
Peaches Cardinal
Basket with Parisienne ice cream
Dessert

From this day in Russian history:

> *Another rainy day. Only during the parade did the sky get brighter. After the liturgy there was a big breakfast for 190 people. The celebrations for Name Day turned out to be dull as poor Alix didn't feel well and stayed in bed until tea time. Read and wrote replies to telegrams. At 4 pm the cruiser 'Kagul' and three battleships, which arrived in Yalta yesterday, passed through Livadia on the way to Sebastopol.*
>
> *At 7.30 pm I had dinner with the ship's company. Then my daughters danced and played on the lower deck while I played dominos in Alexei's cabin. In the evening the weather cleared because of the fresh northerly. Returned home at 12.30.*
>
> From the Diary of Nicholas II

ଔଞ୍ଚ

On 8 December 1913 the Russian Riviera newspaper reported in great detail on the public celebrations marking the Emperor's Name Day. Special services took place in all the churches and cathedrals of Livadia and Yalta. Many representatives of the Russian and other European Courts and High Society attended all the celebrations. There were military parades and naval salutes to add to the joyous ceremony of the day. A grand firework display closed the day's activities. The Shirvansky choir of the 84th Infantry Regiment provided music and singing to accompany the day's pageantry.

> *The Sovereign Emperor dressed in the uniform of the Guard Crew and wearing the ribbon of St Andrew inspected all the troops and*

offered his greetings for the special day, after which he raised a charka of vodka to toast all those units present. Major General Dumbadze then invited everyone to toast the health of the Imperial Family.

CRPO

Fire in the House of Aivazovsky

In Feodosia, for some unknown reason, the house, in which the famous artist Aivazovsky was born and lived, burned down.

There was nothing left of the building apart from the bare walls. The house had been insured with the Moscow Society for 4,000 roubles. Everything was lost in the fire with the exception of a commemorative plaque.

Russian Riviera, 6 December 1913

CRPO

Salute from the vessels of the Black Sea Navy, Livadia, 1912. Photo by Gun.
From the photographic archives of the Yalta Museum of History and Literature.

Puréed Soup
(serves 2)

Ingredients:
200 g (½ lb) beef bones
2 carrots
200 g (3 cups) cauliflower
1 bulb celeriac‡
1 onion
200 g (1½ cups) kohlrabi‡
50 g (⅓ cup) wheat flour
1 egg yolk
1 tbsp melted butter
60 ml (¼ cup) milk‡
Salt and pepper to taste
1 bunch mixed herbs of choice, chopped finely
500 ml (2 cups) water

Cooking method:
Prepare the stock by putting the bones in the water and bringing to the boil. Turn down the heat and continue to simmer gently. Meanwhile, prepare the vegetables. Wash them thoroughly, scrape the kohlrabi and then cut everything into cubes or, if you prefer, grate coarsely. Boil in salted water until soft. Drain the vegetables and sieve or liquidize. Mix the flour in a little water, then add the puréed vegetables, milk and some of the herbs and stir into the strained stock. Now add the egg yolk mixed with the melted butter. Stir well. Bring carefully to the boil, whilst continuing stirring. When ready, sprinkle with the rest of the herbs and serve with toast.

Soup à la Tortue
(serves 2)

In the days of Count Leo Tolstoy, Soup à la Tortue was indeed made from the meat of green turtles. However, as time went by, there was an increasing tendency to use the 18th century English recipe for mock turtle soup. This was of course a much cheaper imitation, using brains and offal to duplicate the texture and flavour of turtle meat. The complexity of these recipes was such that they would be almost impossible to reproduce in a modern kitchen. The following recipe, whilst still being of some complexity, can, however, produce a soup not dissimilar in texture and taste.

Ingredients:
225 g (½ lb) piece of shoulder of veal on the bone
1 calf's head
2 chicken breasts
1 tsp salt
Freshly ground black pepper
25 g (¼ cup) grated Parmesan
Grated nutmeg to taste
1 egg
200 ml (1 cup) double cream[‡]
Mixed root vegetables
100 g (½ cup) black olives, stoned
50 g (⅓ cup) potato flour (or plain flour, if potato flour is not available)
25 ml (5 tsp) oyster sauce
60 ml (¼ cup) Madeira
Cayenne pepper

Cooking method:
For the stock, cut the shoulder of veal into medium-sized pieces and sauté until slightly coloured.

Place the veal bones in a deep saucepan and cover with water. Add the sautéed meat and simmer for up to 2 hours until the stock is well coloured.

Remove the tongue and brains from the calf head. Boil the head and tongue in unsalted water and the brains in a little salted water.

Cut the chicken into small cubes and chill for 30 minutes. Then place this chicken, salt and pepper, Parmesan, a little nutmeg and the egg in a food processor. Blend thoroughly, adding the cream a little at a time until the ingredients are thoroughly mixed and smooth. Bring a saucepan of water to the boil. Adjust the heat so that the water is simmering and add spoonfuls of the mixture, allowing them to poach until cooked. This will take 6 minutes or so. When ready, remove these quenelles and place in cold water.

Cut the selection of vegetables into large pieces and boil in salted water.

Rinse the boiled calf's head in cold water. Remove the ears and chop into medium-sized pieces. Place the pieces in a clean saucepan, together with the vegetables, quenelles and olives.

Cut the brains into small pieces and add to the mixture. Now sieve the stock and add to the pan. Bring everything to the boil twice, skimming off any froth thus produced. Mix the potato or plain flour with 100 ml (½ cup) cold water, adding it to the soup while stirring quickly to prevent the formation of any lumps. Add Madeira, oyster sauce and a little cayenne pepper.

Jellied Sterlet à l'Impériale
(serves 4)

Ingredients:
1 kg (2 lb) sterlet‡
1 medium-sized carrot, 1 parsnip and a similar sized piece of celeriac‡, chopped
1 onion, chopped
15–20 g (6 tsp) gelatine
Pieces of crayfish‡ or crabmeat to serve
A few sprigs of parsley to garnish

Cooking method:
Clean and wash the sterlet and dry with kitchen roll (paper towel). Cut into pieces. Simmer for 10–15 minutes together with the vegetables and onion. Remove the pieces of sterlet from the stock and place them in a deep dish or salad bowl and cover with kitchen paper. Add the gelatine, previously soaked in water, to the stock and stir carefully until fully dissolved. (In olden days, homemade gelatine would have been clarified by using caviar.) Bring the stock to the boil, remove from the heat and allow to stand for 5 minutes. Sieve through a fine mesh. Leave to cool, then pour over the fish. Decorate with parsley leaves, crayfish or pieces of crabmeat.

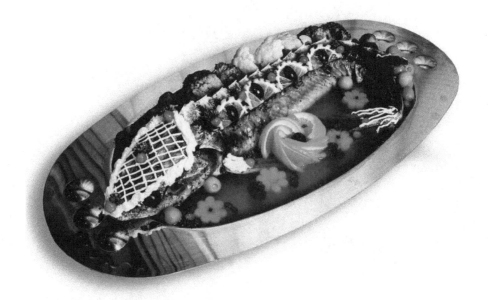

Jellied Sterlet à l'Impériale

Veal Roast
(serves 1[50])

Ingredients:
2 veal chops
Salt
Ground black pepper
200 ml (1 cup) vegetable oil
3 medium potatoes
1 onion
1 carrot
Ground nutmeg
Crushed coriander‡ seeds
250 ml (1 cup) beef stock

Cooking method:
Rub salt and pepper into the chops and seal them quickly in hot oil, using a heavy pan. When ready, transfer to a plate. Slice the potatoes thickly, sprinkle with salt and then fry in the same oil. When ready, strain and remove. Now cut the onion and carrots into circles and fry them in the oil. Place these fried vegetables on top of the potatoes and sprinkle with a little ground nutmeg. Take the chops, sprinkle with some crushed coriander seeds and then place on top of the vegetable mixture. Carefully add the stock, pouring it slowly down the sides of the pan. Cook gently over a low heat for 30–40 minutes.

---

[50] One with an Imperial appetite, or perhaps two lesser mortals!

Roast Spring Chicken Stuffed with Mushrooms
(serves 4)

Ingredients:
2 spring chickens‡
300 g (4 cups) mushrooms‡
75–100 g (½ cup) lard‡
Salt to taste
Pepper to taste
Paprika to taste
8 slices speck‡ (if unobtainable, use thin slices of very fat bacon‡)

Cooking method:
Preheat oven to 180 °C / 350 °F.

Wash the chickens through and pat dry. Sprinkle with salt. Chop the mushrooms finely and fry them in lard. Add salt and sprinkle with paprika. Stuff the chickens with this mixture. Cover with thin slices of speck/bacon and secure with string. Roast in the oven until cooked. Remove the slices of speck and return the chickens to the hot oven and allow to crisp. Serve with fried potatoes.

Stuffed Duck in Sauce Périgueux

Stuffed Duck in Sauce Périgueux
(serves 6)

Ingredients:
300 g (⅔ lb) veal, minced (ground)
300 g (⅔ lb) pork, minced (ground)
3 eggs
1 onion
1 sprig of thyme
230 g (2⅓ cups) shallots
250 g (3 cups) Brussels sprouts
1.5 kg (3⅓ lb) boned duck
500 g (2½ cups) foie gras[51]
Salt and pepper
Vegetable oil
300 g (2¼ cups) salsify‡

For the Sauce Périgueux:
200 g (2 cups) porcini mushrooms (use 2 canned truffles if available)
50 g (2 oz) butter
250 ml (1 cup) light stock
50 ml (¼ cup) Madeira

Cooking method:
Preheat the oven to 175 °C / 350 °F.

Combine the veal, pork, foie gras, eggs, chopped onion and thyme. Peel the shallots and salsify and prepare the Brussels sprouts. Stuff the duck with the prepared meat mixture and place on a baking tray. Sprinkle with salt and pepper, pour vegetable oil over the top and bake for one hour. After 20 to 30 minutes arrange the vegetables around the duck.

For the sauce:
Chop and fry the mushrooms/truffles. Heat the stock, bringing to the boil whilst whisking lightly. Add the mushrooms and simmer on a very low heat for 10 minutes, stirring constantly. Add wine and simmer until the sauce thickens.

Take the duck out of the oven and leave to stand for a while. Cut into pieces. Serve with the warm sauce.

---

[51] Those wanting to avoid foie gras can find a variety of alternatives online.

Peaches Cardinal
French cuisine
(serves 6)

Ingredients:
300 g (1½ cups) granulated sugar‡
400 ml (1⅔ cups) water
6 ripe peaches
250 g (2 cups) raspberries
50 g (½ cup) flaked almonds
Icing sugar‡
1 kg (3½ pints) vanilla ice cream

Cooking method:
Dissolve the granulated sugar in the water over a low heat, using a deep pan. Skin the peaches, cut them in half and remove the stones. Add the peaches to the syrup, with the cut sides down. Cover with a lid and simmer over a low heat for 10 minutes. The peaches should be cooked until soft but must retain their shape. Remove the peaches from the pan, drain, and place them in a glass bowl.

Purée the raspberries and add to the syrup, in which the peaches have been cooked. Bring back to the boil, skim any froth and simmer over a low heat for 5 minutes. Leave to cool. Toast the almonds in a separate pan.

To serve, use individual glasses, into each of which place two scoops of ice cream and two peach halves. Pour over some raspberry syrup and sprinkle with the flaked almonds.

Peaches Cardinal

French Style Ice Cream
(serves 6)

Ingredients:
50 g (½ cup) freshly ground / instant coffee (adjust according to taste)
120 ml (½ cup) water
120 g (1 cup) caster sugar‡
6 egg yolks
500 ml (2¼ cups) double cream‡

Cooking method:
Dissolve the coffee in 60 ml (¼ cup) of boiling water and put to one side. Now dissolve the sugar in the remaining water, bringing to the boil in a metal dish, and stirring until the syrup is thick enough not to drip off the end of a fork. Push the egg yolk through a sieve. Now pour the syrup onto the eggs very slowly, stirring continually to form a thick mixture. Strain the coffee into this mixture and stir thoroughly. Leave to cool. Whisk the cream and when thick combine with the syrup.

Place the prepared mixture in a freezer and leave it to set. When ice crystals start to form whisk it again for a minute. Place back in the freezer.

As soon as the ice cream has set, it can be served in small pastry baskets. Decorate with fruit.

For pastry baskets:

Basic shortcrust pastry
200 g (1½ cups) flour‡
Pinch of salt
110 g (4 oz) cold butter, cubed
50–75 ml (¼ cup) very cold water

Place the flour and salt in a bowl. Rub in the butter working as quickly and as lightly as possible. Add the water and stir with a cold knife until a good dough is formed. Wrap in cling film and chill for at least 15 minutes before needed.

Roll the pastry into a sheet 5–7 mm thick. Line metal pastry moulds with it and bake the baskets at 200 °C / 400 °F for 15 minutes.

French Style Ice Cream

THE IMPERIAL FAMILY'S FAVOURITE DISHES

From photographic holdings of the Livadia Palace Museum.

Golden Cream Cheese Fritters with Raspberry Jam

Cream cheese fritters with jam was Nicholas II's favourite dish. At Court they were cooked using the Old Russian recipe with full cream cottage cheese and extra currants.

(serves 2)

Ingredients:
25 g (2½ tbsp) currants
300 g (1⅓ cups) cottage cheese
75 g (½ cup) flour‡
1 egg
50 g (½ cup) caster sugar‡
Salt to taste
100 ml (½ cup) vegetable oil
100 ml (½ cup) sour cream‡
50–75 g (3 tbsp) raspberry jam‡

Cooking method:
Wash the currants in cold water. Rub the cottage cheese through a sieve and add half the flour. Whisk in the egg and then add the currants and sugar. Add salt to taste and stir thoroughly. Take this mixture and roll out until about 5 cm (2″) thick. Cut into round slices. Dip each slice in the rest of the flour and shape them into small, flattened buns. Heat the oil in a frying pan and fry the fritters until golden brown. Place them on a large dish and top each with a spoonful of sour cream and a little raspberry jam.

Golden Cream Cheese Fritters with Raspberry Jam

Royal Gateau 'Victoria'
English cuisine – Victoria Sponge
(for 12 slices)

Ingredients:
175 g (1½ cups) icing sugar‡
175 g (¾ cup) softened butter
4 separated eggs
100 g (⅔ cup) flour‡
1 tbsp baking powder
100 g (1 cup) ground almonds
A few drops of almond extract
125 g (1 cup) raspberries

For the filling:
225 ml (⅔ cup) double cream‡
125 g (1 cup) raspberries

For decoration:
2 pink roses
250–285 g (1⅓ cups) icing sugar‡
1 egg white, whisked

Cooking method:
Crystallize the rose petals a day in advance. To do this, separate the rose petals. Take one petal at a time and, using a very small brush, cover one side with egg white. And, using no more than 85 g of the icing sugar, sprinkle each petal in turn with this icing sugar, shaking off any excess. For this it is best to hold the petal with tweezers. Lay the sugared petals on greaseproof paper‡ and leave for 24 hours.

To prepare the cake:
Grease two medium-depth 20 cm (8″) cake tins with butter and line with greaseproof paper‡. In a bowl whisk the icing sugar and softened butter until light and fluffy. Add the egg yolks. Now add the sieved flour and baking powder. Mix everything together with a large metal spoon, adding the ground almonds and the almond extract. As soon as the flour has been smoothly incorporated, stop mixing. Whisk the egg whites until fluffy. In order to keep the cake mixture as light as possible, fold in a third of the whites at a time. Now carefully add 125 g (1 cup) of raspberries to the mixture and divide it between the prepared tins. Smooth the tops with a spatula. Bake for 30–35 minutes in an oven preheated to 180 °C / 350 °F.

When cooked, remove from the oven and allow to rest for 5 minutes before turning out onto a cooling rack.

Decoration:

Place one layer on a serving dish. Cover with whipped double cream and sprinkle this with 125 g (1 cup) of raspberries. Carefully place the second cake layer on top of the filling. Using 30 ml (2 tbsp) of cold water, mix the icing sugar until a paste-like consistency is achieved. If too runny, simply add a little more icing sugar. Colour lightly with a little pink food colouring and spread carefully over the top and sides of the cake. Place the crystallized rose petals on top and dust with icing sugar.

Royal Gateau 'Victoria'

Gurievskaya Kasha

Recipe 1
(serves 6)

This particular version of kasha is named after Count Dmitri Alexandrovich Guriev (1751–1825), who was the Minister of Finance under Alexander I. While his financial reforms did not survive for posterity, this recipe remains *au courant*!

Note:
Semolina porridge can be aromatized as follows:
Add cloves and grated orange peel when the milk comes to the boil.
Add currants, pre-soaked in rum for a few minutes, before the end of cooking.
Several cardamom pods can also be added to the milk while it is being heated.

Ingredients:
100 g (1 cup) walnuts
100 g (⅔ cups) cashew nuts
100 g (½ cup) granulated sugar‡
200 g (1⅓ cups) currants
600 ml (2½ cups) single cream‡
200 g (1 cup) semolina
250 g (1¼ cups) strawberries
200 g (1⅓ cups) blackberries
Sufficient butter for greasing the mould and the plates used for laying cream skins

Cooking method:
Combine the nuts. Chop three quarters of the mixture and reserve. Put the remaining whole nuts in a tray lined with silver foil and place for 12 minutes in an oven preheated to 150 °C / 300 °F.

Meanwhile put the chopped mixture in a frying pan together with 30 g (2½ tbsp) of sugar and 18 ml (1 tbsp) of water. Heat the pan and stir until the mixture caramelizes.

Cover the currants with boiling water and leave for 10 minutes.

Pour the single cream into a large shallow pan and bake it in the oven at 200 °C / 400 °F (if using a fan oven, turn off the fan or this will prevent the skins from forming) until a good skin is formed. Remove this skin with a slotted spoon and place it carefully on a flat buttered plate. Repeat this procedure four more times, each time putting the skin on a separate plate. When cool, cut one skin into wide strips.

Bring the remaining cream to the boil in a saucepan. Start whisking and add the remaining 70 g (5⅔ tbsp) of sugar and the semolina. Add the pinch of salt and cook over medium heat, stirring constantly until thick.

Combine the semolina mixture with the strips of one skin, the berries and caramelized nuts. Mix together well.

Mix most of the berries with the caramelized nuts, reserving a few berries for decoration.

Using a spatula, spread a layer of this porridge over the bottom of the mould and smooth down. Next comes a layer of the nuts and berries mixture, over which place a layer of the skins. Repeat this procedure covering the final layer of porridge with sugar. Place the completed mould in the oven and bake at 170 °C / 340 °F until the top caramelizes. Remove the mould from the oven and carefully turn out the kasha onto a serving plate. Decorate with the reserved berries and nuts.

Recipe 2 (Old Style)
(serves 6)

Ingredients:
500 ml (2 cups) milk‡
Salt to taste
100 g (½ cup) semolina
1 egg, separated
100 g (½ cup) sugar‡
1 deseeded vanilla pod
50 g (½ cup) walnuts, chopped
600 ml (2½ cups) single cream‡
50 g (2 oz) butter
10 apricots, stoned
50 g (½ cup) walnuts, finely chopped

Cooking method:
Preheat oven to 150 °C / 300 °F.

Bring the milk to the boil, add a little salt and gradually stir in the semolina. Cook until it turns sticky. Cool the kasha a little and then add the egg yolk mixed with the sugar, whisked egg white, vanilla and the (roughly chopped) walnuts after frying them in butter. Thoroughly mix everything together.

Pour the cream into a small pan and place in the preheated oven until a skin forms. Each time a skin forms, remove it with a slotted spoon and place each skin on a separate dish to cool, then cut into strips.

Grease an oven-proof dish. Place alternate layers of kasha, chopped apricots and the skin strips, finishing with a top layer of kasha. Increase the temperature of the oven to 180 °C / 350 °F and cook the kasha until golden brown. Remove the dish from the oven and sprinkle with the 50 g (½ cup) of finely chopped walnuts. If wished, pour some walnut or apricot liqueur over it.

Gurievskaya Kasha

INDEX OF RECIPES

Drinks

Notes on ingredients

Dairy

Cream – Single	Unsterilized cream with 18% milk fat.
Cream – Double	With a minimum of 48% milk fat this whips easily and thickly.
Cream – Sour	Smetana is produced by souring heavy cream, and generally has 10% to 40% milk fat. Its cooking properties are different from lighter American sour creams (12–16% fat) and crème fraîche (28% fat), as it neither curdles nor melts.
Milk	Russia has countless varieties of milk, but the type envisaged in the recipes here would be cow's milk with 3–6% fat.
Buttermilk	Effective substitutes include plain yoghurt or soured milk (produced by adding vinegar or lemon juice to milk).

Vegetables

Celeriac	A turnip-rooted or knob celery cultivated for its edible roots – also known as 'celery root' in some areas.
Celery	A vegetable with a firm stalk (composed of multiple 'ribs') and leafy ends.
Coriander	If referring to the leaves, also known as cilantro.
Cos lettuce	Also known as Romaine lettuce.
Curly endive	Also known as frisée or (in some areas of the US) chicory, this is the spindly leaf type of lettuce – not the wide-lobed escarole, nor the closely-packed white Belgian endive also known as 'sugarloaf' or (in the UK) chicory.
Green beans	Unripe beans, consumed with their pods: known in some areas as 'French beans'. See 'runner beans'.
Kohlrabi	A 'turnip cabbage', with a mild flavour and crunchy texture.
Mangetout	Also known as snow peas (or sometimes sugar snap peas).
Mushrooms	Unless otherwise noted, champignons (button mushrooms).
Runner beans	Ripe beans, normally consumed without pods: also known in some areas as 'green beans' (but see above).
Salsify	A lesser known root vegetable also known as oyster plant.
Spring onions	Also known as green onions or scallions.
Sweet pepper	Also known as bell pepper, capsicum or pimiento.

Meat

Capon
: A rooster that has been castrated before reaching sexual maturity. Capon meat is relatively fatty, tender and flavourful.

Poularde
: A fattened young chicken, the female equivalent of a capon. Note that although one recipe given here says 'rooster or poularde', roosters are quite different from poulardes, and to confuse matters further, poulard (no 'e') can mean 'roaster' – q.v. https://en.wikipedia.org/wiki/Poularde. If unavailable, capon is an acceptable alternative.

Spring chicken
: A small, young chicken, sometimes referred to as 'poussin' or 'Cornish hen' (but definitions vary with area).

Pork Fat
: Hard fat cut from under the skin of a pig's back with or without the skin.

Speck
: Cured pork belly with a juniper flavouring.

Bacon
: Cured meat from the back or side of a pig, sliced thinly; differentiated from streaky bacon (from the belly).

Lard
: Rendered or unrendered pig fat with uses similar to butter.

Fish

Crayfish
: Also known as crawfish, crawdads, freshwater lobsters, mountain lobsters, mudbugs, or yabbies.

Gurnard
: A fish that lives on the seabed, also known as the sea robin.

Prawn
: For our purposes, the same meaning as shrimp.

Ruffe
: A small and invasive freshwater perch, no longer found in the market but increasingly common in the wild.

Sterlet
: A small type of sturgeon, used for caviar. As sturgeon is now a vulnerable species due to overfishing, halibut is a better substitute.

Miscellaneous

Biscuit
: Equivalent to cookie or Graham cracker, depending on context.

Caster sugar
: Also known as superfine / ultrafine / extra fine / berry / fruit / bar / instant dissolving / fondant sugar.

Cornflour
: This is the extracted starch derived from raw maize kernel, not the dry ground flesh of the whole kernel. Also called masa harina or cornstarch; not to be confused with American corn flour (fine corn meal, i.e. maize flour, a finer ground version

of cornmeal / polenta), or Australian cornflour (powdered starch, which can be derived from wheat instead).

Flour	Unless otherwise noted, plain (wheat) flour, also known as all purpose (AP) flour.
Granulated sugar	Common variety.
Icing sugar	Also known as powdered or confectioner's sugar, or icing sugar *mixture* (includes anti-caking agent, to prevent clumping).
Jam	A sweet preserve, known in some areas as 'jelly' (q.v.).
Jelly	A gelatine-based dessert, known in some areas as 'jello'.
Paper	Greaseproof paper is also known as parchment paper or baking paper.
Stock cube	Also known as 'bouillon cube'.

Notes on weights & measures

Units vary so much over time, only a few arbitrary examples are provided here – those interested can find more online. For instance, 1 garnets can be anything between 2.75 and 7.12 kg or litres, depending on area and historical period.

		1 chetvert	8 chetverik		209 kg (or l)
64 lbs	2 buckets	1 chetverik	8 garnets	26 kg	
32 lbs	1 bucket	½ chetverik	4 garnets	13 kg	
8 lbs	¼ bucket	4 quarts	1 garnets	3.2 kg	
3 lbs	6 glasses	1.5 quarts / 1 shtof		1.2 kg	
2 lbs	4 glasses	1 quart	¼ garnets	800 g (or ml)	
1 lb.	2 glasses	16 tablespoons	32 lots	400 g	
½ lb.	1 glass	8 tablespoons	16 lots	200 g	
	⅛ glass	1 tablespoon	2 lots	25 g	
		½ tablespoon	1 lot	12.8 g	

Modern equivalents can also be quite diverse: for example, a 'tablespoon' can refer to anything from 7 to 25 ml, depending on country, etc. We have adapted the recipes in the interests of readability, but some experimentation may be needed to get the balance right!

Oven temperatures:

°C (fan)	°C	°F	Gas
90	100		
100	110	225	0.25
110	120	250	0.5
120	130		
130	140	275	1
140	150	300	2
150	160	325	3
160	170		
170	180	350	4
180	190	375	5
190	200		
200	210	400	6
210	220	425	7
220	230		
230	240	450	8
240	250	475	9
	260	500	10

Biographies
(in order of first name)

- ### Alexander Alexandrovich Mosolov (1854–1939)
Chief of the Office of the Ministry of the Imperial Court, last ruling General and Chief of Staff of the Ministry of the Court and Principalities (1902–1917). Major General, Head of the Office of the Ministry of the Imperial Court envoy to Romania. He was on the Board of the post-revolutionary Union of United Monarchies. Author of the book '*At the Court of the Last Tsar*'.

- ### Grand Duke Alexander Mikhailovich of Russia (1866–1933)
Alexander Mikhailovich, also known as Sandro, was a childhood friend and close advisor to Nicholas II, and his first cousin once removed. Although his career lay principally with the Russian Imperial Navy, one of his passions was wine-making – alongside writing and architecture. The Grand Duke's Crimean estate at Ay-Todor produced both red and white wines: Burgundies, Pedro Ximénez, Sémillon, Cabernet Sauvignon, Sweet Muscat and Madeira.

- ### Anna Semionovna Nebolsina (1798–1850)
She was married to Ivan Alexeyevich Nebolsin whose ancestry can be traced to the 15th century. The motto of this noble family was 'Devotion and Love to the Faith and Homeland'. Representatives of the family included prominent scientists, writers, artists, military leaders and statesmen of exceptional eminence.

- ### Boris Matveyevich Sokolov (1889–1930)
A literary scholar and folklorist, he was one of the writers of the 'Tales and Songs of the Belozerskii region' (1915) and of the 'The Poetry of the Village' (1926). In the 1920s he conducted an expedition to Saratov to study the ethnology and folklore of its peoples, including the Chuvash. Sokolov established the ethnographic museum in the city of Saratov and was the first director of the Central Museum of Ethnology. He was secretary of the magazine 'Ethnography' from its inception in 1926 and wrote more than 40 scientific works.

- ### Prince Daniel von Buchau (1546–1608)
German Ambassador extraordinary and plenipotentiary in Russia

- ### Dmitri Alexandrovich Guriev (1751–1825)
A Russian statesman, Minister of Finance, a Member of the State Council and a Count from 1819, Guriev outlived his political career but his name lived on. His

taxes and duties in the wine trade were long known as the Guriev monopoly. Although these have now been all but forgotten, his name endures because of his creation of the famous Russian dish Gurievskaya kasha (see p.158).

- **Feodor Feodorovich Raskolnikov (1892–1939)**

A Bolshevik whose real name was Feodor Ilyin. He was a leading participant in the October Revolution, Commander of the Red Navy in both the Caspian and the Baltic during the Russian Civil War and later became a Soviet diplomat. The pseudonym Raskolnikov most probably came from Rodion Raskolnikov, the fictional protagonist in Crime and Punishment, the novel by Feodor Dostoevsky.

- **Count Feodor Vasilievich Rastopchin (1763–1826)**

The Count was a Russian statesman who served as governor of Moscow during the French invasion of Russia.

- **Friedrich Wilhelm von Bergholz (1699–1765)**

His father was a Holstein nobleman and a general in Peter I's Russian army, which meant that Friedrich spent most of his youth in Russia. When his father died in 1717 Friedrich returned to Germany where he became a companion to the Duke of Mecklenburg and, later, an attendant to the Duke of Holstein-Gottorp, Charles Frederick, whom he accompanied on trips to Paris and Stockholm. In 1721 Duke Charles Frederick came to St Petersburg in a bid to marry Anna, the daughter of Peter I. Friedrich accompanied him and was promoted to the position of usher to the Duke (who did succeed in marrying Anna in 1726). From this time until 1725 Friedrich kept an amazingly detailed diary that is now regarded as the best archival source about life in the court of Peter I and his final years as Tsar.

- **Georgi Konstantinovich Zhukov (1896–1974)**

Marshal of the Soviet Union and a career officer in the Red Army. During World War II he played a pivotal role in leading the Red Army's drive through Eastern Europe in its attempt to liberate the Soviet Union and other nations from German occupation. He contributed ultimately to the taking of Berlin. He was the most decorated officer in the history of the Soviet Union and Russia.

- **Giles Fletcher (1548–1611)**

Fletcher was an English poet, diplomat and MP born in Watford, Hertfordshire. The son of a vicar, he spent his early life in Cranbrook, Kent before he became a pupil at Eton College around 1561. From there, Fletcher continued his education at King's College, Cambridge where he gained his BA in 1569. He studied Greek and poetry, and rose through the ranks of academia to become Dean of Arts at King's

College in 1581. Following his marriage, he gave up his fellowship and decided to study for a Civil Law degree. He settled back in Kent and had a child, Phineas. He was elected to parliament in 1584 to represent Winchelsea (a Cinque Port) and in 1588 became ambassador to Russia to re-establish a treaty with Tsar Feodor I. Fletcher published 'Of the Russe Commonwealth' in 1591. He hoped to engender more trade between Russia and England and Queen Elizabeth I made him a Master of Requests. He produced a vivid account of Russia prior 1600. His most famous sonnet is *Licia*, and both Phineas and his second son Giles Fletcher the Younger became poets.

How Giles came to the Russian court

Tsar Feodor of Russia (1557–1598) was the son of Ivan IV (The Terrible), and he was the last Rurikid Tsar of Russia. He has been called Feodor the Bell ringer because of his strong religious faith and love of ringing church bells. He was known for his extreme piety. He was crowned Tsar in 1584 following the death of his elder brother Ivan Ivanovich. Feodor was notorious for openly contradicting his father and refusing to maintain exclusive trading rights with England. He wished to open Russia to all foreigners and did, in fact, send Sir Jerome Bowes, the pompous British ambassador back to England. This led Elizabeth I to send in a new ambassador, Giles Fletcher the Elder. His job was to persuade Boris Godunov, Feodor's brother-in-law, to convince the Tsar to return to the old, special arrangement with England. Fletcher was, however, reputed to have wrecked the negotiations after inadvertently addressing Feodor by the wrong title. This left the English Queen no alternative but to write letters herself to try to retrieve the special alliance between the two nations. Feodor refused to budge regarding his decision but as the years went by he eventually handed over governance of the country to his brother-in-law, Boris. Some historians say Feodor was simple minded. He only had one child, a daughter, who died aged two and when he himself passed away in 1598, the Rurik dynasty died with him. He was buried in the Cathedral of the Archangel in the Moscow Kremlin. He was succeeded by Boris Godunov.

- ### Prince Grigori Alexandrovich Potemkin (1739–1791)

A Russian military leader, statesman, nobleman and favourite of Catherine the Great, Prince Potemkin died during negotiations over the Treaty of Jassy that ended a war with the Ottoman Empire that he had overseen.

- ### Ivan Andreyevich Krylov (1769–1844)

A Russian writer, fabulist and academician of the St Petersburg Academy of Sciences, Ivan published the satirical magazine 'Letters from the spirit world' (1789) and wrote tragedies, comedies and opera libretti. Between 1809 and 1843 he produced more than 200 fables, imbued with the spirit of democracy and written in lively yet thought-provoking language with some satire. While many of his earlier fables were loosely based on Aesop's and La Fontaine's texts, the later ones were original works often satirizing the incompetent bureaucracy that was responsible for stifling social progress during his time. His fables exposed social and human vices, and Gogol called the fables "…a book of common wisdom."

- **Johann Gottlieb Georgi (1729–1802)**

A German chemist, botanist, naturalist and geographer who was also a Professor of Mineralogy, Johann was native of Pomerania. Georgi accompanied both Johan Peter Falk and Peter Simon Pallas on their respective journeys through Siberia. Between 1770 and 1774 he travelled on behalf of the Imperial Academy of Sciences to Astrakhan, the Urals, Bashkir, the Barabinsk steppe, the Kolyvanskoye silver mines, Altai, Tomsk, Irkutsk, Baikal, and Dauria (Transbaikal). In 1783 he became an Academician of the Russian Imperial Academy of Sciences in St Petersburg.

- **Konstantin Petrovich Pobedonostsev (1827–1907)**

A Russian jurist, statesman, and advisor to three Tsars, Konstantin is usually regarded as the prime representative of reactionary views after the death of Alexander II and was the 'éminence grise' of imperial politics during the reign of Tsar Alexander III. He was the main Procurator in the Holy Synod in its relations with the Russian Orthodox Church.

- **Larisa Mikhailovna Reisner (1895–1926)**

A Russian writer best known for her participation in the Russian Civil War following the October Revolution. She was the wife of Feodor Raskolnikov and the mistress of Karl Radek, an active Marxist and participant in international Communist movements between 1904 and 1939.

- **Lavrenti Pavlovich Beria (1899–1953)**

Chief of the Soviet security and secret police (NKVD) during World War II. He played a major role in the mass repressions in the Soviet Union under Joseph Stalin and was responsible for the death of millions of Soviet people. Beria was executed in 1953 on charges of rape and treason.

- **Maurice Paléologue (1859–1944)**

A French diplomat, historian, and essayist.

- **St Olga, Christian name of Yelena following her baptism (c.890–969)**

She ruled Kievan Rus' after the death of her husband, Prince Igor Rurikovich from 945 to 962. The first of the Rus' rulers to convert to Christianity and one of the first Rus' people to be proclaimed a saint.

- **Count Pavel Konstantinovich Benkendorff (Paul Leopold Johann Stephan Gr. von Benckendorff) (1853–1921)**

A marshal of His Majesty's Court from 1893 to 1912, the Count became Chief Marshal from 1912 to 1917. He was also a member of the State Council of the Russian Empire from 1916 to 1917.

- **Pierre Jules Theophile Gautier (1811–1872)**

This French poet, dramatist, novelist, journalist and art and literary critic was an ardent defender of Romanticism and widely admired by writers as different as Baudelaire, Flaubert, Oscar Wilde and Proust. His passion for travel led him to Russia and his travelogues are considered by many academics as among the best written in the 19th century. He published Trésors d'Art de la Russie in 1858 and Voyage en Russie in 1867.

- **Semyon Mikhailovich Budyonny (1883–1973)**

A Russian cavalryman, military commander during the Russian Civil War, Polish-Soviet War and World War II, and a close political ally of Soviet leader Joseph Stalin.

- **Sergey Mikhailovich Solovyov (1820–1879)**

Sergey was one of the greatest Russian historians, and his influence was paramount on the next generation, a generation that included Vasily Klyuchevsky, Dmitri Ilovaisky and Sergey Platonov. His eldest son Vsevolod Solovyov was a historical novelist and another son, Vladimir, was one of the most authoritative Russian philosophers.

- **Tatyana Kirillovna Okunevskaya (1914–2002)**

Soviet and Russian actress. Honoured artist of the Russian Socialist Federal Republic (1947).

- **Vasily Alexandrovich Naschokin (1707–1760)**

Lieutenant General Naschokin kept a record (in the form of a diary) between 1712 and 1759 that reflected the family and social events that he attended or heard about.

- **Vasily Sergeyevich Sheremeteff (1752–1831)**

The great nephew of Count Sheremeteff and a field-marshal for Peter I. Major General Sheremeteff was the governor of Izyaslav and Volyn provinces and was awarded the Orders of St Anna of the 1st degree, and St Vladimir of the 2nd degree.

- **Vasily Vasilievich Kamensky (1884–1961)**

Vasily Kamensky was a Russian futurist poet, playwright, and artist as well as one of the first Russian aviators.

- **Prince Vitovt the Great (c.1350–1430)**

One of the most famous rulers of the Grand Duchy of Lithuania.

- **Baron/Count Adolf Andreas Woldemar/Vladimir Borisovich Frederiks/Freedericksz) (1838–1927)**

Russian statesman, minister of the Imperial Court (1897–1917) and a member of the State Council of the Russian Empire (1905).

- **Prince Vladimir Sviatoslavich the Great (c. 958–1015)**

Prince of Novgorod and Grand Prince of Kiev, ruler of Kievan Rus' (980–1015)

- **Yakov Mikhailovich Yurovsky (1878–1938)**

A Bolshevik, best known as the chief executioner of Tsar Nicholas II, his family and four retainers on the night of 17 July 1918.

- **Yevgeny Nikolayevich Opochinin (1858–1928)**

A contemporary and young friend of Dostoevsky, he was the author of 30 books and many publications for various newspapers and magazines. In 1887 he successfully published a book about the history of Russian theatre. He also wrote a leading essay entitled 'How the plots of Dostoevsky's novels were taken from Real Life'.

- **Yevgeny Vasilievich Bogdanovich (1829–1914)**

Infantry general and writer of monarchist literature. In 1888 he was promoted to Privy Councillor and appointed member of the Council of the Minister of the Interior.

- **Princess Zinaida Ivanovna Yusupova née Naryshkina (1809–1893)**

Maid of honour, Russian aristocrat, socialite and the great-grandmother of Felix Yusupov, the Princess was responsible for the intricately styled Baroque interiors of the family Palace on the Moika in St Petersburg. She also initiated many other buildings in the city and the famous family dacha in Tsarskoye Selo.

Bibliography

A.A. Mosolov, 1935. *At the Court of the Last Tsar.* St Petersburg: Methuen.

A.K. Baiburin, A.L. Toporkov, 1990. *At the root of etiquette.* Leningrad: Nauka.

G. Konstantinovich, 2001. *Memories in the Marble Palace.* Moscow: s.n.

N. Matveyev, 1912. *Moscow and Moscow life before the 1812 invasion.* Moscow: s.n.

N.A. Yepanchin, 1996. *At the service of three Emperors.* Moscow: s.n.

O.Y. Zakharova, 2003. *The power of ceremonies and ceremonies of power in the Russian Empire of the XVIII - early XX century.* Moscow: Argumenty i Fakty (AiF) Print.

P.A. Viazemsky, 1883. *Complete set of works.* Volume 8 ed. St Petersburg: s.n.

P.V. Romanov, 2000. *The feast history of the Russian state.* St Petersburg: Kristall.

S.P. Zhikharev, 1980. *Notes of a contemporary. Diary of a student.* Volume 1 ed. Leningrad: s.n.

S.V. Yurchenko, 2005. *Yalta Conference, 1945: The Chronicles of the Creation of the new World.* Simferopol: s.n.

T. Okunevskaya, 2001. *Tatiana's Day.* Moscow: s.n.

V.A. Sollogub, 1988. *Stories. Memoirs.* Leningrad: s.n.

V.L. Vinogradova, 1967. *Reference of Terms for 'The Tale of Igor's Campaign'.* Leningrad: Nauka.

Y.M. Lotman, E.A. Pogosiyan, 1996. *High Society Dinners Panorama of Metropolitan Life.* St Petersburg: Pushkin.fond.

Y.S. Riabtsev, 1998. *The anthology of the history of Russian culture in the 18th and 19th centuries.* Moscow: s.n.

About the Authors

The original Russian version of this book was the result of a collaboration between Sergey Pushkaryov and Oksana Zakharova and was published in 2007. In 2012, the book received a further boost from reviewers when the Moscow publishing house Tsentrpolygraph published a revised and enlarged edition under the new title '*The Russian ceremonial feast: original menus and recipes from the Imperial kitchens of the Livadia Palace*'.

Oksana Yurievna Zakharova is a Doctor of Historical Sciences and a Professor at Lomonosov Moscow State University. She is a renowned specialist in the ceremonial culture of Imperial Russia, having authored or co-authored 49 articles, 32 books, 14 conference reports, 11 dissertations and 7 training courses.

Sergey Nikolayevich Pushkaryov was born in Moscow in 1954 and graduated from the Donetsk State University in 1976 with a degree in Philology. He has been actively involved in the establishment and work of a local history museum in the town of Chernomorskoye and the Association of Crimean Nature Reserves & Museums, and has authored over 60 academic articles on a variety of subjects, including the history of church buildings and old estates.

Marina George was born in Voronezh in 1960. Following the completion of a Master's Degree in English Language and Literature at the Voronezh State University in 1986, Marina gained a Diploma in Translation and Interpreting and, after acquiring valuable working experience, went on to work as a freelance translator and interpreter. She is a fully qualified member of the Institute of Translation and Interpreting and a member of the National Register of Public Service Interpreters.

Provender: Memories of Imperial Russia in Kent

Some of the Russian Imperial Court did escape the revolution, the Grand Duchess Xenia Alexandrovna and Grand Duke Alexander Mikhailovich being amongst those rescued from Crimea by British gunboats. It is their granddaughter Princess Olga Romanoff, who has written the Foreword to this book.

The Princess currently lives near Faversham in Kent at Provender House. The site has both strong ties with the history of the Russian Imperial Family and reflects much of England's own history during the last seven hundred years. Having housed adventurers, explorers, heiresses and princesses, its rooms represent a fascinating record of English architecture of Medieval, Tudor, Jacobean, Queen Anne, Georgian and Victorian times.

Provender is situated in thirty-six acres of the Kentish countryside at Norton, near Faversham.

John de Provender is the first recorded owner of a property there during the reign of Henry III (1154–1189). It would appear to have been a classic example of a medieval aisled house, with two transepts and although only one of them has survived, it is still regarded as one of the finest specimens of its type in Britain.

The transepts were created to contain service rooms on one side of the house, and more luxurious accommodation for the family on the other. Since then, it has been added to throughout the centuries and now only a few beams and trusses of the original house survive. The de Viennes, who acquired the house in the 14th century, added a private wing, complete with a magnificently vaulted solar with carved crown posts, which is the pride of Provender today.

The continuing process of adding to, and adapting, the house has resulted in a unique, architectural experience. Exploring the house now is rather like an architectural journey through more than seven hundred years of English history.

Many different families have occupied the house over the years. In 1633, for example, Provender was sold to James Huguessen, a merchant adventurer, whose descendants continued to live there for nearly three hundred years. In March 1779 a later female descendant, Dorothy Huguessen, married naturalist Sir Joseph Banks, well-known for his role as the botanist on Captain Cook's voyage to the South Pacific, and it was he who planted the chestnut trees and Banksian roses. As no children resulted from this marriage, the house was subsequently inherited by Dorothy's nephew, Edward Knatchbull-Huguessen, 9th Baronet and the first Lord Brabourne.

It was around this time that Jane Austen most likely visited Provender, as her brother lived not far away, in Godmersham. It is tempting to think that Jane saw in Lord Brabourne a potential husband for her favourite niece Fanny Knight, who did in fact become Edward's second wife. Her son edited the first edition of Jane

Austen's letters, which he had found in a box at Provender along with an original copy of Jane Austen's early novel, Lady Susan, in the author's own hand-writing.

Sylvia McDougall, the grandmother of the present owner, Princess Olga Romanoff, bought the house from the Knatchbull-Huguessens in 1912. When Olga's father, Prince Andrei Romanoff married Olga's mother, Nadine McDougall in 1942, it became their home. However, during the war, the house was requisitioned by the army and often used as a base by Field Marshal Montgomery, so the couple had to move into a rented property nearby.

After the war, in 1949, they moved back and began the gargantuan task of thoroughly rejuvenating the building and its extensive gardens (Olga's grandmother had tried to carry out significant repairs, but many of these had been sadly ill-judged and responsible for much further decay.)

When her father, a nephew of Nicholas II, escaped the Russian revolution with his pregnant wife and his father Grand Duke Alexander Mikhailovich of Russia (Sandro) in December 1918 on HMS Forsyth, he had managed to bring with him various items from the Imperial Court. It was money from sale of these that contributed to the restoration of the house.

Provender was Prince Andrei Romanoff's only real home in exile. He spent his time gardening, painting, entertaining and even cooking, which he had learnt from the French chefs in his parents' palaces. Born in 1950, Princess Olga grew up at Provender, so it became her great wish to restore the gardens, for she remembers so well her father's love of the grounds and especially the walled kitchen garden. She recalls how he always said that the English grew the best vegetables – although by the time English cuisine had boiled them to death, you would never have known!

Today, Princess Olga shows visitors around the house, and relates many more of her father's stories about life as a member of the Russian Imperial Family. There are many historic photographs, portraits, and pieces of furniture on show, including a desk that once belonged to Queen Alexandra, wife of Edward VII. Another poignant item is a rare pre-Revolution bottle of wine, from the family's Crimean estate of Ay Todor, which belonged to her grandfather, Grand Duke Alexander (see photo on page 8).

Following a grant in 2003 from English Heritage, Princess Olga and her three children have been involved in a serious restoration project, working closely with conservation architect Ptolemy Dean. Slowly but surely, and driven by the Princess's determination, this amazing house has been restored to some of its former glory. Everything possible is being done to ensure maximum authenticity throughout the 33 rooms. Mr Dean was passionate about the project and followed the work of the skilled and traditional craftsmen with great enthusiasm. Close attention has been paid to every aspect of historical and architectural detail, even to the level of the correct colour for the 18th century mouldings in one of the bathrooms.

Princess Olga hosts large events including weddings at Provender and she continues to welcome visitors who are keen to learn more about the house and the Imperial Russian heritage of her family.

Opening times and further information on Provender can always be obtained by visiting www.provenderhouse.co.uk.

OTHER PUBLICATIONS FROM ŌZARU BOOKS

Ōzaru Books is a boutique publisher based in the Thanet village of St Nicholas-at-Wade. Our primary focus is on books with a local connection, ranging from creative writing by East Kent authors to (occasionally niche) scholarly tomes about Kentish history, but we have a secondary interest in works in translation, particularly from Eastern languages, and also tales from East Prussia. Some of our profits go to support gorilla charities, which is the origin of the name Ōzaru ('Great Ape') and our logo.

Discordant Comicals
– The Hooden Horse of East Kent –

George Frampton

DISCORDANT COMICALS
The Hooden Horse of East Kent
George Frampton

Hoodening is an ancient calendar custom unique to East Kent, involving a wooden horse's head on a pole, carried by a man concealed by a sack. The earliest reliable record is from 1735, but other than Percy Maylam's seminal work "The Hooden Horse", published in 1909, little serious research has gone into the tradition.

George Frampton has rectified this, by cross-referencing dozens of newspaper reports, census records and other accounts to build a comprehensive picture of who the Hoodeners were, why (and where) they did it, and how it related to other folk traditions.

He then goes beyond Maylam to look at the 'demise' of Hoodening in around 1921, its widely heralded 'revival' in 1966, and discovers that this narrative is in fact quite misleading, as several Hooden Horses were still active throughout that period. He includes descriptions of the current teams, and supplies plentiful appendices detailing past participants, places visited, songs performed, events on Hoodening's timeline, and the horses themselves.

Full indices make it easy for modern Men and Maids of Kent to check whether their ancestors might have been involved, and detailed references make this an invaluable resource for social historians too.

The book features over 70 full colour illustrations.

"a good read for the interested layman as well as a valuable resource for anyone interested in the custom" (The Morris Dancer)

"very readable research [...] backed up with generous quotations [...] reveals a tale of rich cultural heritage." (The Living Tradition)

"thoroughly researched [...] well presented [...] full of previously un-published interviews [...] in depth analysis [...] extremely interesting" (Around Kent Folk)

"provides a sense of the scope and history of the rarely studied practice of hoodening [...] offers the most up-to-date and comprehensive starting point for any scholar interested in the practice" (The Journal of Folklore Research)

"attractively published in hardback with numerous colour illustrations [...] A lot of admirable spadework and academic endeavour [...] copious references are given throughout" (Master Mummers)

"Frampton has left no stone unturned in his research [...] there is a very useful index, which helps make this a book to dip into profitably" (Archæologia Cantiana)

"profusely illustrated and printed in colour, it's a treat for the eyes [...] meticulous and detailed [...] a compelling and intriguing volume" (Tykes' News)

ISBN: 978-0-9559219-7-3

The Margate Tales

Stephen Channing

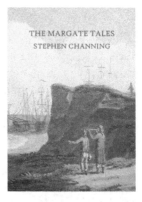

Chaucer's Canterbury Tales is without doubt one of the best ways of getting a feel for what the people of England in the Middle Ages were like. In the modern world, one might instead try to learn how different people behave and think from television or the internet.

However, to get a feel for what it was like to be in Margate as it gradually changed from a small fishing village into one of Britain's most popular holiday resorts, one needs to investigate contemporary sources such as newspaper reports and journals.

Stephen Channing has saved us this work, by trawling through thousands of such documents to select the most illuminating and entertaining accounts of Thanet in the 18th and early to mid 19th centuries. With content ranging from furious battles in the letters pages, to hilarious pastiches, witty poems and astonishing factual reports, illustrated with over 70 drawings from the time, The Margate Tales brings the society of the time to life, and as with Chaucer, demonstrates how in many areas, surprisingly little has changed.

"substantial and fascinating volume...meticulously researched...an absorbing read" (Margate Civic Society)

ISBN: 978-0-9559219-5-7

Turner's Margate Through Contemporary Eyes
– The Viney Letters –

Stephen Channing

Margate in the early 19th century was an exciting town, where smugglers and 'preventive men' fought to outwit each other, while artists such as JMW Turner came to paint the glorious sunsets over the sea. One of the young men growing up in this environment decided to set out for Australia to make his fortune in the Bendigo gold rush.

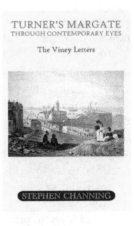

Half a century later, having become a pillar of the community, he began writing a series of letters and articles for Keble's Gazette, a publication based in his home town. In these, he described Margate with great familiarity (and tremendous powers of recall), while at the same time introducing his English readers to the "latitudinarian democracy" of a new, "young Britain".

Viney's interests covered a huge range of topics, from Thanet folk customs such as Hoodening, through diatribes on the perils of assigning intelligence to dogs, to geological theories including suggestions for the removal of sandbanks off the English coast "in obedience to the sovereign will and intelligence of man".

His writing is clearly that of a well-educated man, albeit with certain Victorian prejudices about the colonies that may make those with modern sensibilities wince a little. Yet above all, it is interesting because of the light it throws on life in a British seaside town some 180 years ago.

This book also contains numerous contemporary illustrations.

"profusely illustrated...draws together a series of interesting articles and letters...recommended" (Margate Civic Society)

ISBN: 978-0-9559219-2-6

A Victorian Cyclist
– Rambling through Kent in 1886 –

Stephen & Shirley Channing

Bicycles are so much a part of everyday life nowadays, it can be surprising to realize that for the late Victorians these "velocipedes" were a novelty disparaged as being unhealthy and unsafe – and that indeed tricycles were for a time seen as the format more likely to succeed.

Some people however adopted the new-fangled devices with alacrity, embarking on adventurous tours throughout the countryside. One of them documented his 'rambles' around East Kent in such detail that it is still possible to follow his routes on modern cycles, and compare the fauna and flora (and pubs!) with those he vividly described.

In addition to providing today's cyclists with new historical routes to explore, and both naturalists and social historians with plenty of material for research, this fascinating book contains a special chapter on Lady Cyclists in the era before female emancipation, and an unintentionally humorous section instructing young gentlemen how to make their cycle and then ride it.

A Victorian Cyclist features over 200 illustrations, and is complemented by a fully updated website.

"Lovely...wonderfully written...terrific" (Everything Bicycles)

"Rare and insightful" (Kent on Sunday)

"Interesting...informative...detailed historical insights" (BikeBiz)

"Unique and fascinating book...quality is very good...of considerable interest" (Veteran-Cycle Club)

"Superb...illuminating...well detailed...The easy flowing prose, which has a cadence like cycling itself, carries the reader along as if freewheeling with a hind wind" (Forty Plus Cycling Club)

"a fascinating book with both vivid descriptions and a number of hitherto-unseen photos of the area" ('Pedalling Pensioner', amazon.co.uk)

ISBN: 978-0-9559219-7-1
Also available on Kindle

Bicycle Beginnings

The Advent of the Bicycle or Velocipede… and what people of the 19th century were really saying about it

Stephen Channing

Cycling is such a natural activity for millions of people around the globe now, it is difficult to imagine that a little over a century ago many regarded it as reprehensible, revolting, or indeed revolutionary. The best way to get a feel for what early 'velocipedists' encountered is to read the words of the times, and this book gathers into one volume the most enlightening, entertaining and extraordinary insights from contemporary sources.

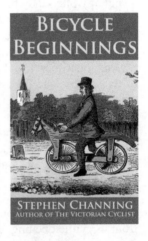

The mammoth work (over 190,000 words, covering the period 1779 to 1912) contains race reports, legal developments, technical innovations and inventions, records, advertisements, acrobatics, clothing, poems, arguments for and against the new-fangled vehicles, debates over women cyclists, and a long travelogue, "Berlin to Budapest on a Bicycle" capturing the excitement of a forgotten age of adventure on two wheels.

Not all the inventions were two-wheeled, however. This book also reveals the numerous variations that came into being before makers standardized on the shapes we commonly see nowadays: tricycles, ice velocipedes, water-paddle hobby-horses... These are explained with the aid of numerous illustrations, covering the gamut from cartoons to technical drawings and photographs. Even the race reports demonstrate far more variety than we are accustomed to seeing: 'ordinaries' (penny farthings) versus 'safety' bicycles versus tandems, monocycles, dwarf cycles, tricycles, double tricycles, four-wheel velocipedes, horses, ice skaters, steamships...

Rather than a single narrative to be read in one go, it is an anthology of fascinating glimpses into cycling's 'golden age', providing a new understanding of a bygone age of experimentation and much amusement, whenever the reader dips into it.

ISBN: 978-1-5210-8632-2
Also available on Kindle

The Call of Cairnmor

Sally Aviss
Book One of the Cairnmor Trilogy

The Scottish Isle of Cairnmor is a place of great beauty and undisturbed wilderness, a haven for wildlife, a land of white sandy beaches and inland fertile plains, a land where awe-inspiring mountains connect precipitously with the sea.

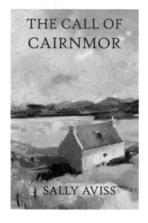

To this remote island comes a stranger, Alexander Stewart, on a quest to solve the mysterious disappearance of two people and their unborn child; a missing family who are now heirs to a vast fortune. He enlists the help of local schoolteacher, Katherine MacDonald, and together they seek the answers to this enigma: a deeply personal journey that takes them from Cairnmor to the historic splendour of London and the industrial heartland of Glasgow.

Covering the years 1936-1937 and infused with period colour and detail, The Call of Cairnmor is about unexpected discovery and profound attachment which, from its gentle opening, gradually gathers momentum and complexity until all the strands come together to give life-changing revelations.

"really enjoyed reading this – loved the plot...Read it in just two sittings as I couldn't stop reading." (P. Green – amazon.co.uk)

"exciting plot, not a book you want to put down, although I tried not to rush it so as to fully enjoy escaping to the world skilfully created by the author. A most enjoyable read." (Liz Green – amazon.co.uk)

"an excellent read. I cannot wait for the next part of the trilogy from this talented author. You will not want to put it down" (B. Burchell – amazon.co.uk)

ISBN: 978-0-9559219-9-5
Also available on Kindle

Changing Tides, Changing Times

Sally Aviss
Book Two of the Cairnmor Trilogy

In the dense jungle of Malaya in 1942, Doctor Rachel Curtis stumbles across a mysterious, unidentifiable stranger, badly injured and close to death.

Four years earlier in 1938 in London, Katherine Stewart and her husband Alex come into conflict with their differing needs while Alex's father, Alastair, knows he must keep his deeper feelings hidden from the woman he loves; a woman to whom he must never reveal the full extent of that love.

Covering a broad canvas and meticulously researched, Changing Times, Changing Tides follows the interwoven journey of well-loved characters from The Call of Cairnmor, as well as introducing new personalities, in a unique combination of novel and history that tells a story of love, loss, friendship and heroism; absorbing the reader in the characters' lives as they are shaped and changed by the ebb and flow of events before, during and after the Second World War.

"I enjoyed the twists and turns of this book...particularly liked the gutsy Dr Rachel who is a reminder to the reader that these are dark days for the world. Love triumphs but not in the way we thought it would and our heroine, Katherine, learns that the path to true love is certainly not a smooth one." (MDW – amazon.co.uk)

"Even better than the first book! A moving and touching story well told." (P. Green – amazon.co.uk)

"One of the best reads this year...can't wait for the next one." (Mr C. Brownett – amazon.co.uk)

"One of my favourite books – and I have shelves of them in the house! Sally Aviss is a masterful storyteller [...She] has obviously done a tremendous amount of research, judging by all the fascinating and in-depth historical detail woven into the storyline." ('Inverneill' – amazon.co.uk)

ISBN: 978-0-9931587-0-4
Also available on Kindle

Where Gloom and Brightness Meet

Sally Aviss
Book Three of the Cairnmor Trilogy

When Anna Stewart begins a relationship with journalist Marcus Kendrick, the ramifications are felt from New York all the way across the Atlantic to the remote and beautiful Scottish island of Cairnmor, where her family live. Yet even as she and Marcus draw closer, Anna cannot forget her estranged husband whom she has not seen for many years.

When tragedy strikes, for some, Cairnmor becomes a refuge, a place of solace to ease the troubled spirit and an escape from painful reality; for others, it becomes a place of enterprise and adventure – a place in which to dream of an unfettered future.

This third book in the *Cairnmor Trilogy*, takes the action forward into the late nineteen-sixties as well as recalling familiar characters' lives from the intervening years. *Where Gloom and Brightness Meet* is a story of heartbreak and redemptive love; of long-dead passion remembered and retained in isolation; of unfaltering loyalty and steadfast devotion. It is a story that juxtaposes the old and the new; a story that reflects the conflicting attitudes, problems and joys of a liberating era.

"the last book in Sally Aviss's trilogy and it did not disappoint...what a wonderful journey this has been...cleverly written with an enormous amount of research" (B. Burchell – amazon.co.uk)

"I loved this third book in the series...the characters were believable and events unfolded in a beguiling way...not too happy ending for everyone but a satisfying conclusion to the saga" (P. Green – amazon.co.uk)

ISBN: 978-0-9931587-1-1
Also available on Kindle

Message from Captivity

Sally Aviss

When diplomat's daughter Sophie Langley is sent on an errand of mercy to the Channel Island of St Nicolas in order to care for her two elderly aunts, she finds herself trapped in an unenviable position following the German invasion.

In the Battle for France, linguist and poet Robert Anderson, a lieutenant in the Royal Welch Fusiliers, finds himself embroiled in an impossible military situation from which there seems to be no escape.

From the beautiful Channel Islands to the very heart of Nazi-occupied Europe, Message From Captivity weaves factual authenticity into the fabric of a narrative where the twists and turns of captivity, freedom and dangerous pursuit have unforeseen consequences; where Robert's integrity is tested to the limit and Sophie needs all her inner strength to cope with the decisions and challenges she faces.

"The structure of the book takes you between the main protagonists and weaves their lives together as the story unfolds, add to that authentic research on the events of the period and you have a great story which keeps you guessing to the end." (P. Green – amazon.co.uk)

ISBN: 978-0-9931587-5-9
Also available on Kindle

The Girl in Jack's Portrait

Sally Aviss

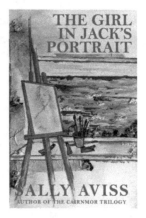

When struggling barrister Callie Martin encounters soldier Jamie Rutherford on ceremonial duty near Horse Guards Parade, her life is changed forever. When Edie Paignton's ex-husband deprives her of alimony, she puts her lovingly restored Victorian house up for sale and finds her life transformed by a chance meeting with architect Ben Rutherford, Jamie's father. When successful businessman Erik van der Waals discovers an unknown name and telephone number on a piece of paper, he determines to meet the owner. And when mental health nurse, Sarah Adhabi, embarks on a dangerous new relationship, she discovers she is more than a match for the new man in her life.

Six people seeking an escape from their pasts; six people seeking redemption in the present; six people who find their lives interwoven and their secrets revealed.

But just who is the Girl in Jack's Portrait?

ISBN: 978-0-9931587-6-6
Also available on Kindle

Reflections in an Oval Mirror
Memories of East Prussia, 1923–45

Anneli Jones

8 May 1945 – VE Day – was Anneliese Wiemer's twenty-second birthday. Although she did not know it then, it marked the end of her flight to the West, and the start of a new life in England.

These illustrated memoirs, based on a diary kept during the Third Reich and letters rediscovered many decades later, depict the momentous changes occurring in Europe against a backcloth of everyday farm life in East Prussia (now the north-western corner of Russia, sandwiched between Lithuania and Poland).

The political developments of the 1930s (including the Hitler Youth, 'Kristallnacht', political education, labour service, war service, and interrogation) are all the more poignant for being told from the viewpoint of a romantic young girl. In lighter moments she also describes student life in Vienna and Prague, and her friendship with Belgian and Soviet prisoners of war. Finally, however, the approach of the Red Army forces her to abandon her home and flee across the frozen countryside, encountering en route a cross-section of society ranging from a 'lady of the manor', worried about her family silver, to some concentration camp inmates

"couldn't put it down...delightful...very detailed descriptions of the farm and the arrival of war...interesting history and personal account" *('Rosie', amazon.co.uk)*

"Anneli did not fully conform but she still survived, and how this happened is the real gem...There is optimism, humour, great affection and a tremendous sense of adventure in a period when this society was hurtling towards disaster." *('Singapore Relic', amazon.co.uk)*

ISBN: 978-0-9559219-0-2
Also available on Kindle

Skating at the Edge of the Wood
Memories of East Prussia, 1931–1945…1993

Marlene Yeo

In 1944, the twelve-year old East Prussian girl Marlene Wiemer embarked on a horrific trek to the West, to escape the advancing Red Army. Her cousin Jutta was left behind the Iron Curtain, which severed the family bonds that had made the two so close.

This book contains dramatic depictions of Marlene's flight, recreated from her letters to Jutta during the last year of the war, and contrasted with joyful memories of the innocence that preceded them.

Nearly fifty years later, the advent of perestroika meant that Marlene and Jutta were finally able to revisit their childhood home, after a lifetime of growing up under diametrically opposed societies, and the book closes with a final chapter revealing what they find.

Despite depicting the same time and circumstances as "Reflections in an Oval Mirror", an account written by Marlene's elder sister, Anneli, and its sequel "Carpe Diem", this work stands in stark contrast partly owing to the age gap between the two girls, but above all because of their dramatically different characters.

ISBN: 978-0-9931587-2-8
Also available on Kindle

Ichigensan
– The Newcomer –

David Zoppetti
Translated from the Japanese by Takuma Sminkey

Ichigensan is a novel which can be enjoyed on many levels – as a delicate, sensual love story, as a depiction of the refined society in Japan's cultural capital Kyoto, and as an exploration of the themes of alienation and prejudice common to many environments, regardless of the boundaries of time and place.

Unusually, it shows Japan from the eyes of both an outsider and an 'internal' outcast, and even more unusually, it originally achieved this through sensuous prose carefully crafted by a non-native speaker of Japanese. The fact that this best-selling novella then won the Subaru Prize, one of Japan's top literary awards, and was also nominated for the Akutagawa Prize is a testament to its unique narrative power.

The story is by no means chained to Japan, however, and this new translation by Takuma Sminkey will allow readers world-wide to enjoy the multitude of sensations engendered by life and love in an alien culture.

"A beautiful love story" (Japan Times)

"Sophisticated...subtle...sensuous...delicate...memorable...vivid   depictions"
(Asahi Evening News)

"Striking...fascinating..." (Japan PEN Club)

"Refined and sensual" (Kyoto Shimbun)

"quiet, yet very compelling...subtle mixture of humour and sensuality...the insights that the novel gives about Japanese society are both intriguing and exotic"
(Nicholas Greenman, amazon.com)

ISBN: 978-0-9559219-4-0
Also available on Kindle

Sunflowers
– Le Soleil –

Shimako Murai
A play in one act
Translated from the Japanese by Ben Jones

Hiroshima is synonymous with the first hostile use of an atomic bomb. Many people think of this occurrence as one terrible event in the past, which is studied from history books.

Shimako Murai and other 'Women of Hiroshima' believe otherwise: for them, the bomb had after-effects which affected countless people for decades, effects that were all the more menacing for their unpredictability – and often, invisibility.

This is a tale of two such people: on the surface successful modern women, yet each bearing underneath hidden scars as horrific as the keloids that disfigured Hibakusha on the days following the bomb.

"a great story and a glimpse into the lives of the people who lived during the time of the war and how the bomb affected their lives, even after all these years" *(Wendy Pierce, goodreads.com)*

ISBN: 978-0-9559219-3-3
Also available on Kindle and Google Books

The Body as a Vessel

Approaching the Methodology of Hijikata Tatsumi's Ankoku Butō

MIKAMI Kayo
An analysis of the modern dance form
Translated from the Japanese by Rosa van Hensbergen

When Hijikata Tatsumi's "Butō" appeared in 1959, it revolutionized not only Japanese dance but also the concept of performance art worldwide. It has however proved notoriously difficult to define or tie down. Mikami was a disciple of Hijikata for three years, and in this book, partly based on her graduate and doctoral theses, she combines insights from these years with earlier notes from other dancers to decode the ideas and processes behind butō.

ISBN: 978-0-9931587-4-2

CPSIA information can be obtained
at www.ICGtesting.com
Printed in the USA
BVHW012207160821
614593BV00002B/27